THE LAST TRAVELS
OF A FAT BULLDOG

THE LAST TRAVELS
OF A FAT BULLDOG

George Courtauld

CONSTABLE · LONDON

First published in the UK 2000
by Constable, an imprint of Constable & Robinson Ltd
3 The Lanchesters, 162 Fulham Palace Road
London W6 9ER

Copyright © George Courtauld 2000

The right of George Courtauld to be identified
as author of this work has been asserted by him in
accordance with the Copyright, Designs and Patents Act 1988

A CIP catalogue record for this book
is available from the British Library

ISBN 0-09-480300-5

Printed and bound in the EU

CONTENTS

CONTENTS

CONTENTS

INTRODUCTION
AND
ACKNOWLEDGEMENTS

There is a large porcelain dish on a table by the front door of my house. It is painted with mythical Chinese figures, is two foot across and weighs two stone. I am particularly aware of this weight as I carried it much of the way from Cat Street in Hong Kong, where I had bought it, to my farmhouse in north Essex. When I arrived home with this enormous and useless platter my wife Dominie had no idea what to use it for or where to put it, until she had an inspiration: it could go by the door for calling cards.

The use of calling (or visiting) cards has almost disappeared, except for very formal occasions or for businessmen and diplomats: one hundred years ago a card was essential equipment for a social visit. It was handed to the butler or maid at the door and was often assessed for its social suitability (for example, was it engraved or only embossed?) and usually kept as an *aide-mémoire* for the household. A code was used: how many cards were left could indicate whether the caller had been accompanied or alone, male or female, married or unmarried; which corner of a card was bent would indicate, for example, that the caller had come with his wife and daughter, but his womenfolk only would call on the lady of the house next time.

As a family, we have lived in this house for five generations: some of the furniture is filled with the accumulation of the Victorian and Edwardian eras, of two world wars, of international tragedies, national celebrations and family anniversaries. Among the clutter, mostly in the drawers of old desks, were collections of cards. I gathered them all together and put them in the Chinese dish. Among the worthy Essex and Suffolk names are exotics, and I have pondered over them: why

[9]

were we visited, for example, by Mme Mathilde Emin Bey of Sebastopol, Dr Heer en Mevrouw Bangert-Bakker of Aerdenhout, Dr Gaspar Geist of Budapest, Ludwig Freiherr von Twickel, La Condesa de Olmos and Wilhelm Karl Viktor Ofenheim Ritter von Ponteuxin. The occasional visitor might still leave a card which can be added to the collection; when I travel I might exchange cards with the people I meet, and they too are put into the dish.

This book, which includes some of my last journeys as a Queen's Messenger during 1997 to 1999, as well as a few holiday trips during that time, also includes memories of people I have met. I have reminded myself of them by picking cards out of my dish, recalling people and friends far away, or disappeared, or dead.

I seem to be able to remember people's conversations, even if I forget their faces or names. I bought a tape recorder from a 'Spy-shop' in New York to record people secretly, but gave it up almost at once because it seemed rather dishonourable to record private chat; also, if people were told that they were being taped, they usually became pompous and stilted, or giggly. Interestingly, when summarising a recording, I found it harder to home in on the phrases and quirks of language which made the speaker memorable. So I have relied primarily on my memory and notebooks. For the sake of people's privacy, I have changed most names of those mentioned (whether alive or dead); but I have not changed titles or occupations or nationalities, for those are intrinsic characteristics that somehow make people different from each other, whether the individual be a docker or a duchess, a colonel or a cardinal, a Turk or a Tibetan.

I am still bound by the Official Secrets Act, so like my two previous books, this, the last of my trilogy of travel as a Queen's Messenger, is about places and people, not about the work. Anyhow, when I tried to make out that I was a combination of James Bond, Biggles and Bulldog Drummond, Dominie would spoil it by pointing out that most of the time I was more like Postman Pat.

I must thank all my travelling companions, particularly Queen's Messengers Peter Allen and Major Michael Senior; also Jack and Betty Couldrey in Kenya, the Revd Peter Ellis in Hong Kong, William and Caroline Courtauld in the Far East, Ricardo and Angelica Badilla in

Chile, Kay Coombs in China (now Ambassadress in Outer Mongolia), Lieut.-Colonel Keith McIntosh in Barbados, 'Rose' in Cuba, and my ever-patient editor, Ruth Thackeray, who once again, with kind good humour, has pointed out my arcane spelling, grammatical quirks, schoolboy jokes, Over-the-Top rants and Politically Incorrect opinions.

1997 December ~ MONGOLIA, Ulaan Baatar

Day 1.

'The mice have stopped up their holes with horse dung instead of stones, the stomachs of slaughtered sheep are black, the marmots have only recently started to hibernate. Therefore although it is already cold it is unlikely to get worse.'

Thus says the weather section of *The UB POST* (Mongolia's weekly English-speaking newspaper): much more interesting than all that technical stuff about isobars and occluded fronts. Actually it is uncommonly mild today, a warmish wind is blowing down the bleak streets of Ulaan Baatar, the patches of snow on the mountainsides are dwindling and two months of frozen gob spat upon the pavements is liquefying. Andrew and I are skidding on it during our trudge down the main street in Ulaan Baatar: the half-hour walk from Sukhe Baatar Square to Greyhound Cottage, the Queen's Messengers' little house in the embassy compound. We have been shopping, me to buy the two dozen postcards I always send from this country – everyone always likes the stamps, and the views of wild camels and mounted shepherds and long, lonely valleys – and Andrew secretly to buy something for our appointment in an hour's time. I am wearing my hat 'Boris' – so called because a slanderous fool of a Queen's Messenger said wearing it made me look like Mr Yeltsin. In a previous reincarnation I suspect Boris's name was something like 'Fido' or 'Rex'. Andrew is in trilby and tweeds. I have known Andrew since he was in his pram. Then, with his bulbous shape and glassy eyes, he resembled a small seal. Now he is more like a missionary: his neatly brushed, greying hair, his lined, ascetic face, his spectacles held in place with a black ribbon, his air of gentle amiability; they produce an effect irresistible to many of the inhabitants of the Third World who hurry up to him and, having beaten him over the head and shoulders, divest him of wallet and watch. He tells me that the last time he was mugged was in Pretoria, twice in two minutes.

The Corps of Queen's Messengers has a small fund which is mainly built up from the pockets-full of foreign coins which we carry at the end of journeys. These are emptied into a large urn in the office. When it is full enough, the coins are sorted out and the proceeds are used for the poor children of Mongolia: the simply poor, of poor families; or the tragically poor, orphans and street children, most of whom have heart-breakingly sad histories. All too frequently parents discover that they have too many children to feed and clothe. They therefore tell the least wanted – usually a three- to six-year-old girl – that she is going to stay with her Uncle Fred in Ulaan Baatar. They trek off to the nearest railway station (which may be over five hundred miles away), pop the child on the train, tell her that Uncle Fred will be waiting for her at UB and wave her goodbye. That is the last she ever sees of her family. There is no Uncle Fred, of course. If she is lucky she is picked up by the authorities, if unlucky by the local Fagin or Artful Dodger and she ends up as part of the packs of infants who live in the relatively warm holes in the ground where the central heating pipes from the power station have to go under roads. Eventually they graduate from thieving to child prostitution, favoured by some of the visiting businessmen and politicians.

At present, we spend our fund on quilted anoraks: we buy the material and a Mongolian woman makes them up for us. Together with the ambassador's wife, Shan Durham, Andrew and I are now helping to distribute some. We have arrived at a kindergarten an hour's drive from the embassy. We enter a long, low shed through the normal double doors into a warm corridor, from that into a room crammed with about forty children sitting in a three-sided formation. They range in age and size from the microscopic, aged three, to the tiny, aged seven. They have round faces with dark little almond eyes. After much hand-shaking and introductions from the female staff, we produce the anoraks. They are red and green so they can easily be identified if stolen, sold or used by the older – and less deserving – members of the community. Andrew and I help the children put them on. Andrew is extraordinarily deft, but I am hopeless. (I only once changed a child's nappy – in Blubberhouses Moor. While I was busy retching the nappy was eaten by a sheep.) As I fiddle and heave and sweat to get the anoraks on, the children are stoically impassive, with as much animation as a pillow being stuffed into a pillow case. One of the children I have zipped into an anorak is already well padded with other clothes. He gets redder and redder and redder until he has to be unzipped to let the steam out.

The children now sit and stare and, as we grown-ups talk, their expressions vary from the worried to the bored. Then there is a kerfuffle while the staff arrange the children into a choir-like position. They sing. 'Ding! Ding! Ding!' the song goes, 'Boom! Boom! Boom!' Even Andrew and I, with our limited Mongolian, get the gist. The children then sit down and resume their stoic expressions.

There is a lot of rustling from Andrew, like a terrier in a barn. On the shopping expedition this morning he had bought two large bags of sweets. Suddenly, from the children, we see animation and smiles.

In the late afternoon we hand out more anoraks in the Steppe Inn, the converted container in the embassy yard which serves as a club-house and meeting place. It is crowded with parents, embassy staff, some people from such charities as Save the Children, and a group of four solemn fellows in suits who turn out to be bankers and suchlike, responsible for doling out international money for causes ranging from the charitable to the commercial.

We move on to the Mad Dog night-club, entering through the double-doored cold-excluding porch into a bleak entrance lobby, small and dusty and echoing, through another door into a bedlam of noise. The scene is obscured by clouds of tobacco smoke but I can discern a large central bar, and tables and chairs scattered at random. The decoration is stark, the barest minimum. The lighting is from a few candles and a phosphorescent bulb in one corner, where a bearded man is twanging thoughtfully at a guitar; in another corner a large table is taken up by a dozen Mongolians. The ever-present Mongolian smells of mutton and damp felt have been added to with the smell of beer, cigarettes and the sickly aftershave scents with which oil prospectors sprinkle themselves in the evenings. There are four of us, Bryn and Margaret from the embassy and the two Queen's Messengers. Three of the important bankers are already here, out of their suits and into the normal kit of heavy jersey and corduroy trousers. They call us over to sit with them and they introduce us to their companions: Mongolian assistants who act as liaison officers between their banks and the Mongolian authorities, they say. It is a remarkable coincidence that all the assistants are female, young and pretty. Someone hands out sheets of paper upon which are typed the words of the choruses which will be sung during the evening.

The phosphorescent light illuminates the collars and cuffs of a man's nylon shirt, an East European's cheap false teeth flash and gnash in an eerie, floating grin.

The bearded man sings a lot, so does an attractive Australian girl wearing tight jeans and a little leather waistcoat.

One of our bankers walks over to the singing corner and sings 'Ole Man Ribber' in a very good bass voice.

A round-faced Scot then takes over and keens 'Won't you gang to the Heelands, Lady Lindsay?'

An Australian, so Australian it is surprising he walks rather than kangaroo-hops, then sings 'Waltzing Matilda'. By the time he is halfway through he is moist-eyed in maudlin sentiment; when he has finished it seems that a third of the room is also blubbing.

Bryn stands up. 'I am Welsh,' he announces, 'and we Welsh are known for singing and rugby.' Derisive cries of 'Wales–7, the Springboks–42' are shouted; even the Mongolians are shouting and laughing. Bryn apparently ignores all this, but his song is so melancholy that I think he has taken it in. He sings in Welsh about someone called Myfanwy.

A small, smiling man recites an extremely funny monologue in a probably politically incorrect Jewish accent on the story of David and Goliath.

Suddenly the Mongolians in the corner burst into song, a cheerful ballad. Above the growling of the men, the women's voices float high, their Rs trilling and rolling in that special way which can make Mongolian women peculiarly alluring. Enthusiastic applause.

Our table is now of a dozen people. Some of the bankers feel they must justify themselves by talking shop, but most of us are talking the normal interesting rubbish one talks when relaxed. I have decided to drink vodka – Ghengis Khan brand – explaining that beer goes straight to my bladder, but perhaps the vodka is stronger than I think as things are getting a bit blurry and the singing and conversation are merging into a babble and everyone is talking and singing at once:

So away, away with rum, by gum! With rum, by gum! With rum, by gum!
Away, away with rum, by gum: that's the song of the Salvation Army!

'. . . and of course you will have special interest in that the cashmere fibre from Outer Mongolia is coarser than the fibre from Inner Mongolia, but longer, so we are trying to get them to blend the different fibres to get a finer yarn than the Inner Mongolians can spin but a softer one than the yarns produced here in Outer Mongolia, so our loans . . .'

Ah for just one more time I would take the North-West Passage
To find the hand of Franklyn reaching for the Beaufort Sea,
Tracing one warm line through a land so wild and savage
And make a North-West Passage to the sea.

'. . . if cows are called Primrose or Buttercup and cats are Tiddles or Fluff, and dogs are Rags or Spot or Rover then what are camels? Why Humphrey, of course. Got it? Humps. Camels. Humphrey, see? I heard that from a feller in Bangkok. No, I tell a lie, it was Phnom Penh – or was it Rangoon? Perhaps it was in that little pub in Pudsey . . . Now, have you heard this one? . . .'

> Rise again, rise again, tho' your heart be broken and life about
>   to end,
> No matter what you've lost, be it home, a love, a friend,
> Like the Mary Ellen Carter, rise again!

'Are you going to sing something you know, or do you want the torch?'

> Where the girls are pretty and the beer is free – emigrate to
>   Australia!
> Land of the brave, land of the free, land of the 27-inch TV

'. . . but in Spain the girls rub in olive oil as a sun lotion.'
'No wonder they smell of paella.'

> Dress me up in me oilskins and jumpers, no more on the
>   docks I'll be seen,
> Just tell me old ship-mates I'm taking a trip mates,
> And I'll see you someday in Fiddlers' Green.

'It's a bad cook who will not lick her fingers.'
'Yea, but still, puppies' ears, stewed!'

> *In Scarlet town, where I was born,*
> *There was a fair maid dwellin',*
> *Made every youth cry 'well-a-way!'*
> *Her name was Barbara Allen.*

'Wotcher mean men who apply aftershave fragrances are a pack of poofy ponces? I'll tear your f . . . ing head off your shoulders, mate!'

We reel back to Greyhound Cottage. All around us the city slumbers: the 200,000 people in their bleak, Russian-built apartment blocks, the other 300,000 in their gers (round tents of felt). It is as silent as the surrounding tundra, the streets are empty but for the occasional roving dog or cow under a tree. The freakish thaw of this morning has gone: the thermometer on the wall by the embassy back door says −25° C.

Day 2. A grey and cheerless early morning. The aeroplane will not be flying back to Peking until mid-afternoon so Andrew and I have decided to visit the Japanese military graveyard: a relic of the Japanese invasion in 1939. It is on a bleak hillside outside the city. At this time of the year its thin fuzz of grass has been grazed down to the gritty grey skin of the steppe. The cemetery has been fenced in with iron railings. Little metal labels mark the rows of graves. Most are bare, one or two must have been visited and have small heaps of stones and plastic flowers added. Crows and choughs creak and wail, a sheep cries, the wind sings a dirge through the railings. A ragged shadow drifts overhead: 'Corpse . . . Corpse!' croaks the raven. That is all that the ghosts have heard in the last sixty years. Silent beneath us lie the unwelcome visitors to this land so far from their home of cherry blossom and gongs. It is one of the most melancholy places I have ever visited. I love coming here.

The airport is pretty basic, yet the lavatory is the most complicated I've seen: a centrally heated seat, jets of water which squirt from different angles, several types of flush, taps and spouts, things to hang on to or haul yourself up with. The passengers from here are always interesting: stocky men with steel teeth and heavy overcoats; bearded emissaries in robes seeking help for their terrorist activities; dry little Japanese businessmen; bewildered tourists. This time I notice a silent gang, maybe Americans – the prettiest female amidst them has those level eyebrows and slightly lantern jaws that the American is evolving. Beside her is a man with a knitted red bobble-hat and a long grey beard.

We hang about in the terminal-to-aircraft bus. 'Why aren't we moving?' grumbles Andrew. 'It's bloody freezing.'

'We're still missing one of the passengers,' I tell him.

'Who?'

'The Garden Gnome – ah, here he comes,' I say, as beard-and-red-hat appears and hurries towards us. He climbs aboard.

'There you are, Poppa!' says the good-looking girl, giving me a nasty and meaningful glare as she says it.

No cheerful small talk about the Mongolian weather with her, I can see.

> *Contessa de Santa Sula*
>
> *Villa Sula*
> *Cannes*

1970 ~ The Riviera. 'I want you to meet one of my oldest friends,' said my French cousin Eugenie. 'It is a shame that she is completely mad, but she was once very beautiful. Her husband owned quite a lot of Tuscany.'

I was led to a corner where a seated ancient was holding court to a small group of male admirers. She was swathed in velvet, sprinkled with diamonds, festooned with pearls and covered with wrinkles. I took her proffered hand and nodded briefly over it.

She spoke: 'Eeee, it's Jim! 'ello Jim.' Her accent was that of Leeds.

'Actually, it's George, actually. George.'

'Loovly to see you again, Jim. How are t' croquet balls?'

'*Croquet* balls?'

'Ay, Jim. We won't forget t' croquet balls, will we? Naughty Jim!'

'No, I suppose not.'

And I haven't.

> *Señor Roberto Sandgrouse*
>
> *'Sandringham'*
> *2234 Rue Flamenco*
> *Rio de Janeiro*

1986 ~ Rio de Janeiro.   It is stickily hot, 33° C, even though it is winter. As I sit under a pavement parasol, sipping beer and politely (I hope) fending off people who want to clean my shoes or sell me roast peanuts in paper cones I inspect the stream of humanity walking, hobbling or jogging past. It has become obvious that there are three stages of adulthood, connected basically but not entirely with chronological age – behavioural age is often another matter. I have divided them up into (Y)oung, (M)iddle and (O)ld and will write down the differences:

Y, bicycling past without holding on to the handlebars,

M, waddling about in a dress that is now too tight,

O, sitting on a bench and staring at nothing,

Y, sitting on the same bench, having his spots squeezed by

Y, a girl,

M, a large fellow in ragged jeans and a T-shirt who comes up and asks me the time. I look at my watch and tell him. He also looks at my watch, admiringly. He asks 'English?' I say 'Yes.' He hesitates, smiles vaguely and moves off. I now wonder if he was a potential mugger who changed his mind for some reason. I remember I was advised not to wear my watch or ring in public. Seven of us have been robbed in the last three years. Craik even got shot at. But people are always shooting at him, I think his red hair annoys them.

O, doddering past, arm-in-arm with

O, another old dodderer,

Y, standing on the beach and doing ostentatious exercises,

M, being ignored by girls while doing the above,

O, a man who comes and sits down by the table next to me. Tall and thin, close-clipped moustache, neatly ironed safari suit revealing wrinkled arms and neck; useless-looking dog on a lead with a tartan collar.

The old man catches my eye.

'British, I take it?' he says.

'Yes.'

'Obvious. Obvious. Can't mistake a well-cut blazer. You can tell, at a glance.'

'Eh, uh.'

'How's Old Blighty?'

[21]

'?'

'Yes. The Old Country. I miss it. Goodness gracious, how I miss it. Particularly the rain, you know. Rains here, of course. But like the buggery. Teems. Not the soothing rains. British complexions, peaches and cream; everyone here is that damned brown. Brown as the nuts. Brazil nuts, ha-ha. I jest. And Cambridge, the Alma Mater. Well, my grandfather's, if truth be told. Came here to build railway lines. Damned fool; should have gone to Chile. Or the Argentine. But, Cambridge. Ah, Cambridge, "And is there honey still for tea?" and so forth. *The Times*, "The Thunderer"; we used to subscribe to it, but somehow it lost touch. No interesting news: obsessed with the Frog and the Hun. Taught the Argies a lesson? I'll say we did! They didn't know what was coming to them. Maggie. Iron Maiden. There you are: peaches and cream, but an iron glove. A glove of absolute iron. But a complexion of cream. And peaches. Rain-washed. British soldier, finest in the world. The navy, of course: the Royal Navy. Sandgrouse.'

'?'

'Sandgrouse, Roberto Sandgrouse: my name. Here's my card. Have you yours?'

'Thanks. By Jove! A Queen's Messenger. Her Majesty, very gracious. Good breeding stock, that Lady Diana Spencer, Her Royal Highness the Princess of Wales. You can tell. At a glance. And peaches and cream. Of course. Made in heaven. That wedding. Fairytale.'

'Going back? Oh. Back. Well, actually, I've never been back home, yet. Born here, you know. But I will, I'll return. Sometime. Before I die.'

JOHN
GNATWREN

Johnny
Gnatwren

1990 ~ Hong Kong. I didn't ask Gnatwren for his card. Unasked, with a condescending demeanour, he handed out the autographed cards to all of us sitting in the bar of the United Forces Sports Club in Hong Kong. I came back from this journey during Wimbledon. Our parrot, whose cage was near the television, kept saying things like 'thirty – forty', 'NO BALL!', 'advantage – Miss Bustlefuzz', 'you can NAAT be serious!!!'

All I knew about Gnatwren was that he was a famous tennis player. Like our parrot, I had seen him playing on the television. For some reason Dominie likes watching Wimbledon; I think it bad enough to watch someone playing games and even worse when the players are charmless and bad-tempered louts. And it makes it doubly worse when they are boastful. If I was a famous tennis player people would be thunderstruck by my modesty.

1997 December ~ CHINA, Peking

Day 2. Kay Coombs takes me to the Food Market. It is like a laboratory in a sci-fi film, tanks and cages full of strange features and creatures: goggle eyes, antennae, fangs, sad little 'ET-go-home' faces, armour-plated bodies, multi-limbed blobs; things that writhe or waddle, slither or swim, creep or crawl; tortoises, toads and turtles, jellyfish, squids, large clam shells that seem to be extruding huge ox-tongues; snakes and eels, sea slugs, a dismembered head of a large fish still gasping and gaping; dogs with their bodies skinned except for the tails, paws and heads; pigs' trotters, chickens' feet and sheep's heads; and a tray full of large chrysalises. Each chrysalis is about the size of a big toe. If you prod them their pointed ends twitch and wriggle. What are they of? How do you cook them? Or do you eat them raw, sticking a pin in each end and then sucking out the contents, as my mother did with raw eggs at breakfast? (Dominie, seeing this for the first time, almost broke off our engagement.)

While I wonder, a young Chinese couple come up. They want to practise their English. In the old days every Chinese hankered after 'The Three Necessities': a wristwatch, a bicycle and a sewing machine. But these two are svelte and well dressed: a personal computer, a Porsche and a microwave oven are more likely their priorities. They come from Shanghai and have been summoned to Peking on some governmental job.

Eventually: 'What are those?' I ask, pointing to the chrysalises.

The youth replies in well-accented English: 'We call them "yung". They are of a sort of a moth.' The girl's accent is not as good as his, but breathily attractive: 'Yess, they are the liddle babies of a thort of big moth, or perhaps a budderfly. We fly them in pig fat, put them in our mouses, and sqwass them with our tongue and spit out the skin. Velly healthy.'

We had a bit of confusion over my interpretation of 'mouses' and when that was clarified she said: 'But talking of mice, in Shanghai we eat something called the Thwee Squeaks: the first squeak is when you pick up a tiny naked baby mouse wiss your chopsticks, the second squeak is when you dip it in sauce, and the third squeak is when you bite it.'

She smiled, and showed the prettiest little row of teeth.

Onto my bicycle, to the open-air market in Panjiayuan-lu. It is commonly called the 'Dirt Market' as it is floored with beaten earth, even the majority of the area under the wide open roof.

There are three zones of activity in the walled enclosure. When I enter, the first zone I see is the relaxing and feeding area, bordered by a line of food cubicles, where noodles are being boiled, sweet potatoes baked and other things being fried. Cauldrons and woks emit clouds of steam – as do the line of refuse bins beside them. Then I walk through the assembly area of waiting porters and their carts, mostly two-wheeled 'floats'. Finally I am in the selling area, divided up into sections for pictures, furniture and general antiques. It is Dickensian: the intense activity, the organised chaos, the engrossment of trade and barter, the milling of the crowd, the babble of bargaining and the laughter. The few people who shove or scowl are middle-aged or old: China is one of the few places in the world where the young, rather than their peers, are the polite ones. The brutalising influence of Maoism is fading.

I buy several things, I don't know why, perhaps because of the pleasure of beating down the seller: six little bowls, each with a different character painted in blue, for Yuan 40 each (about £3), a plate from ¥800 to ¥200 ('Sung Dynasty', they said, most unlikely, but very attractive, earth-coloured with a swirly-spirally character in the centre), a tri-sectioned portable wooden shrine with three little figures, ¥1200 to ¥200 (it is quite hideous, now I even resent that 200), a Tibetan *tang* (stick carved with Buddhist symbols and deities) from ¥1400 to ¥250, and a large hand-painted scroll of a tiger for my grandson Ranulf, who admires tigers and whose birthday is soon.

I am musing over another *tang* in a Tibetan stall when I see an extraordinary object close to two drinking cups made of human skulls set in silver: it is boat-shaped, a bit larger than the skulls, white, with a curious pattern in blue leather patches; suddenly I realise it is the left foot of the stall-holder, clad in a 'Trainer' shoe.

A mousily sweet, middle-aged American woman nudges me: 'Tell me, sir, do you reckon this antique vaze any good, these dragons round the edge are kind-a cute. This lady who's selling it says it is Yuan Dynasty?'

'Still hot from the kiln,' I reply. 'I've been told "buy if you like it, not to make money".'

She's got the bit between her teeth, when I pass her next she seems to have bought most of the stuff in front of her and is haggling over the stall-holder's knitting.

Back in our hotel, sitting with Andrew in the lobby with a couple of hundred other tea or beer drinkers, listening to the thirty members of the Central Opera Theatre Orchestra. It is warm and cosy, made more so by the sight, through the huge plate-glass window, of the trees and bushes of the garden being thinly sprinkled by snowflakes. Heavens to Betsy! It's *those* Americans again, bearing down upon us, beaming. When we were introduced by a mutual friend Mrs American said, in a bossy but arch Boston twang: 'George, I must warn you, my hobby is collecting *people*.' Sure enough, they've brought their family photographs, as previously threatened: three children, all teeth, goggle eyes, gingery hair like pigs' bristles and frightful, floppy clothes, some worn back-to-front. If I had such an unattractive family I'd hardly want to record the fact, far less lug the evidence halfway round the world; and even if I'd done that I'd keep it hidden in my wallet, not brandish it about under the noses of strangers.

Day 3. We are in the embassy mini-bus, on the way to Peking airport: I will be supervising the safe departure of Andrew and the diplomatic mail, or 'dipmail', on the British Air London flight; after that I stay here for a couple more days, then on to Hong Kong for two days before my flight home. The back of the bus is packed with a quarter of a ton of dipmail, collected from Hong Kong, Tokyo, Mongolia and China. There are five of us: two Queen's Messengers, two escort-porters from the embassy, Mr Cao Cao (Oddjob) and Mr Ching (The Fixer) and the driver who thinks he is competing in the Monte Carlo rally.

> One for sorrow, Two for joy,
> Three for a girl, Four for a boy,
> Five for silver, Six for gold,
> Seven for a secret never to be told,
> Eight for heaven, Nine for hell,
> Ten the tolling of a sexton's bell,
> Eleven for the—?

What's the next line for a number of magpies?

So – sixteen magpies in the poplar trees between the embassy and the airport terminal; about the only bird left in China after the Great Murderer ordered that all birds be killed, as they were not good communists. No-one touched the magpies, because it is unlucky to kill one; also they probably don't taste very good. Why do they grow so much poplar? My chopsticks often smell of poplar wood, perhaps the whole lot gets made into chopsticks. I notice that sheep are grazing among the plantations with no apparent problems of ring-barking. My sheep would have killed all these trees within a month. Their trunks are painted white for the first four feet, perhaps that is some sort of anti-gnawing stuff. Does it also repel rabbits? Is it worth finding out? I could import it . . . think of all the willow plantations in England which could be opened up for sheep grazing . . . it would be good for the trees also . . . I'll try to find out . . . I feel car sick . . .

Before Andrew checks himself into his aeroplane I have to go into the terminal building to tell the British Air staff various things. The place is packed. I walk past the Duty Free. Among many exotic things they are selling are:

TEA
to help find your lost
Youth & Beauty

*

SHAOXING HUADIAP WINE
A scientific analysis shows that it
contains 21 kinds of Amino Acids, 8
kinds of Sugar and many kinds of
vitamins. Drinking regularly and to
the proper amount will whet your
appetite and prolong your life, too.

*

LUIGI LIQUEUR
Ingredients:
White Wine, Rice, Tortoise,
Plastron Glue, Deer Bone Glue,
White Sugar, Liquorice, Cape Jasmine,
Radix Angelica, China Wolfberry Fruit.
Directions: Direct Oral Consumption.

One's eyes home in on that 'Tortoise', somewhat.

Andrew has boarded the British Air 747; the dipmail has been loaded into the hold; I am standing in the shade of the tail wing, near the main runway, with my escorts. All around us the airport is like a great harbour, with the craft afloat on a sea of concrete. Aircraft zigzag from place to place like the water traffic between Hong Kong and the mainland: buses ferry their complements of passengers from buildings to the aeroplanes, convoys of container boxes are towed by tug-like tractors, vans tack from bay to bay, cars with flashing lights on their roofs speed like motor boats, there are mobile steps not unlike dredgers, here is a lorry ploughing along like a barge, a police-car-cum-patrol-boat zooms past its stern, then an ambulance and two fire engines, nothing urgent, they just like to cruise about, petrol tankers are long and sleek, cargo carriers thunder along leaving clouds of black fumes. A great hulk appears and wobbles its way past me, its bows looming over the little tug which is towing it. It is manoeuvred into its mooring; its gangway is lowered; hatches are opened. From afar, the tail fins of other moored aeroplanes look like the sails of yachts lined up for the start of a regatta. An Air China 747 screams towards us, then swerves off down the perimeter runway. It is followed by the elegant shape of an Airbus 330, the Dragonair logo of a red dragon looking like a sea serpent as it writhes up the white tail. A nearby 737–300, having battened down her hatches, begins to move off. And so they come and go, their names, some more exotic than others, painted on their flanks: Air Volga, China Yunnan Airways, KLM, Zhongyuan Airlines, United Airlines, China Northern, China Eastern, China South West Airlines, Air Great Wall, Dragonair, China Xinhua, Swissair, Air France, Xiamen Airlines, Shandong. . . .

Day 4. Tien-an-men Square is very different from its dour bleakness when I was first here thirteen years ago. Now, even in winter, there are pretty girls in pretty dresses. The small children wear a multi-coloured variety of clothes, not the drab of Mao blue or khaki of pretend soldiers' uniforms. The middle-aged people must be sick with resentment at their wasted adolescence, marching about in ant-like hordes, ugly and angry. But now there are beggars. Many are children, dirty, but as fat and round as pumpkins. One scuttles out of a crevice like a cockroach and dives a hand into my pocket. I fend him off from the top of his close-cropped head: it is prickly and sticky, a bit like the chin of a half-shaven man who has been dribbling on oranges, an entirely new texture. Here is a burnt man, holding out the appalling bundles of contorted twigs which once were fingers; a cripple, slouched on a bench, dozing, a half-smile on his lips – walking tall and free and

handsome in his dreams; a man weaving toys from strips of bamboo –
birds, butterflies, crickets and beetles bob on the end of wands he has
put in a bottle, nodding and dancing as if they were alive.

There is a huge queue to see Mao's corpse; I am tempted to join to
ensure that he is really dead. The instructions on the Monument to the
Peoples Hero's (*sic*) include:

~ The Presenting of Wreaths, Garlands and Small Flowers must
be given 5 days warning to the Tien-an-men Square Admin-
istrative Committee.
~ No Spitting.
~ No Joking.

I lean over the balconies in the side areas of the Forbidden City and look
at the deserted courtyards below, their flagstones grassy; even the roofs
of yellow pantiles sprout weeds. Once, this place was teeming with life,
'looking like heaven, smelling like hell'. Here the women shuffled on
their mangled feet, eunuchs swanned about in their beautiful robes and
their frightful stink of body odour. I look through the dusty windows
into the living quarters of the concubines and officials. Apart from the
unkempt neglect – dusty furniture and ragged textiles – the basic
impression is of opulent discomfort: the beds look as hard as station
platforms, but are draped in beautiful brocades; the chairs are cushioned,
but the sitter has to sit bolt upright; furniture is meticulously jointed, but
the loosely fitting doors and windows must admit screaming draughts.
The ornaments are among the most perfectly crafted in the world, but
there are many I do not like. I do not like cloisonné for a start, nor do I
like the little flowering trees and shrubs made from semiprecious stones.
If it was not all so rich and rare it would be called 'kitsch'. What is bad
taste? I read a whole book on the subject once and it came to no
conclusion except that possibly simplicity is 'good' taste and fussiness
'bad'. But then how would you define a Turkish carpet or a Grinling
Gibbons panel? Still, some civilisations seem to have good taste (the
Ancient Egyptians and Philadelphia Colonial, for example) and others
bad (the France of Louis XIV, Red-Russian Civic).

I have been sitting on a wide stairway scribbling down these musings and suddenly realise that I am all alone. I stroll off to the main gateway. I am the last person out, after a pair of soldiers. The gates are being swung shut by three men: they make irritable gesticulations of the 'hurry up' kind. I ignore them and continue to saunter. The gestures become impatiently aggressive. I saunter slower. As I approach I see that they have started to smile, whether in resignation, or reluctant admiration, or in case a man so insubordinate might be important, I do not know. One even pats me on the back as I step out, but the door booms shut behind me with a defiant sound.

Sophie-Anne Partridge

BBC
BBC World Service
[Education Department]
Portman Square
London

1994 ~ Warsaw to London flight. Miss Partridge, my neighbour, is thirtyish, pretty, clever, witty (well, she laughs at my jokes). She goes round the world teaching English. Her most interesting classes, she says, are when Italians and Chinese are together: one side naughty, noisy and extrovert, the other side prim, well behaved and very, very committed; no hostility, just bursts of giggling at each other.

A stewardess joins us and I ask who are the most difficult people to deal with. She says for boorish manners probably the Japanese, French and Germans, in that order, but a woman can beat a man in rudeness and arrogance any day, although men are more frightening if really badly behaved; drunks worry her less than the persistently amorous.

I tell her that the best put-down I have heard was from an exceptionally pretty stewardess on a Pakistan International Airlines flight: A cocky and slightly drunk lout in the Second Class: 'Hello darling, will you marry me?'

Stewardess: 'I am thanking you sir, very much indeed, but I am already engaged to three people in First Class.'

PETER PEEWIT

Riddled a Vous

No. 1, Silkwinders Road
Leeds

1989 ~ Islamabad to Karachi flight.   By the look of him, the man sitting next to me was some sort of mercenary soldier on leave: burly, a close-shaven head with a thick neck, very fat earlobes and a gold ring in one of them, short-sleeved shirt disclosing tattooed arms, well-polished shoes below well-ironed cotton trousers. He turned out to be a restaurateur.

'Canapés?' asked the air hostess, offering a tray bearing slivers of damp cardboard upon which had been placed the excremental products of a variety of small animals.

'No thank you,' I replied.

'Not hungry?' my neighbour asked.

'That thing she's pushing is not known as "the Typhoid Trolley" for nothing. Pakistan is the only place in the world where I get gyppy tummy, and I've analysed my problem to the meals on this flight.'

He was interested; we talked of food. He owns a restaurant. It is used by a mixed clientèle: businessmen for lunch; undergraduates and adolescents in the evening. He is in Pakistan to recruit cheap labour: 'Trouble is, you get them back home, and they succumb to TB and the next thing you know is that they're convalescing in some expensive nursing home in the Wharfedale. And no stamina, weedy, some of

[31]

them are so thin you'd find more meat on a butcher's pencil. But they learn quick, work hard and don't grumble.'

He told me a recipe of minced-up sole, baked in a coddling dish, with a spoonful of caviar hidden in the middle. As I am allergic to caviar it would not suit me, but Dominie might be interested. Another of his recipes is to simmer gooseberries in elderflower cordial until *al dente*, cool, mix with champagne and gelatine, eat when jellified.

Hiram H. Bunting

~

23, Welkstall Street
Harwich

1956 ~ *Costa Brava.*   As a youth I had a period of inverted snobbery when I presumed that 'roughing it' was the only way to travel. Off I went in T-shirt and shorts and with rucksack to Yugoslavia and bits of the Mediterranean and it suddenly dawned on me that I was usually bored and miserable: my dominant priorities had become where to eat, where to excrete and where to sleep. I also became obsessed with bedbugs, persistently suspecting them to be staring at me from cracks in ceilings, patiently waiting for me to fall asleep before they made their wingless way down to suck my blood. Another priority was keeping away from people who were either dangerous, diseased, sexually peculiar or professionally boring. I met several travellers who were bumming their way around with no specific aim but to keep alive and on the move, and surprisingly their conversation was often dull, unduly focused on themselves, their motivations, their ideals and 'you-must-think-me-mad' personal quirks:

'Hi! I'm "Hi" – I answer to "Hi!" or any loud cry, such as "Fry me!" or "Fritter-my-wig!" That's from Lewis Carroll, you know – his real name was Charles Lutwidge Dodgson. "Dodgy" Dodgson, I say – fancied little girls, you know. Keen amateur photographer. So call me

Hi, short for Hiram. Hiram Bunting. And who are you, if I may be so bold, and what are you doing in Sunny Spain?'

My response was terse.

'So. Hi George. You're waiting to start your National Service! I'd opt out if I were you. I have. Left the rat race. I was getting on quite well in Neasden & Bogall's, promotion almost inevitable – well, apart from any last-minute efforts – effing efforts – by the head of sales, a real bastard, not that there's any thing wrong with being a bastard, I'm one myself, well, he had it in for me because I was not quite his class, you know, and so I thought, this is a rat race and I'm one of the rats, so I'm opting out. Just left. I follow the sun: Spain – sunny Spain – in the summer, maybe Casablanca – charismatic Casablanca – in the winter, get a cheque from my mother now and then – stupid old cow – she said a man who had left the rat race was merely a rat who'd lost his race, she never understood, it's all her fault really. I always had a disadvantage with a name like Hiram, people at school called me a Kraut, but really my father was American, a GI. Got killed before he was able to get married to my mother, she says. They'd be amazed to fits if they saw me now: all living in their "little boxes, little boxes, little tweedle dee, little twiddly dum and they all look just the same", you know it?'

When I finally managed to shake him off he solemnly handed me his card. Poignant, I thought, and sad, but I still do not know why.

1998 February ~ SOUTH AFRICA

Day 2. I am based at Pretoria. Yesterday I flew to Cape Town. Tomorrow I fly to Gaborone and the day after to Lilongwe. These two journeys will be merely there-and-backs in the same aeroplane, but I had six hours in Cape Town. I had time to wander the streets of the governmental area, cobbled and flagged and bounded by graceful white-painted official buildings before meeting Antonia Malan, Professor of Anthropology, as arranged. She, another female professor and I went to Kirstenbosch, the botanic gardens, and had a picnic, surrounded by palms and flowers. An exhibition of Zimbabwean stone carving had been dotted about artistically on the lawns and in the glades: eerie substitutes for garden gnomes. Someone had written an indignant letter in a local paper saying that one of them was revoltingly obscene, but we couldn't find it, though the professor's imagination thought so on occasions.

We talked of peculiar things and I said I was making a list of the oddest things I've seen, ranging from a plastic sjambok to President Washington's false teeth and a necklace of humming-bird skulls; Antonia said that one of the oddest but somehow most expected thing she'd seen was a present given by Jonas Savimbi, terrorist leader in Angola, to P.W. Botha, apartheid President of South Africa: it was a machine-gun carved from ivory. To add to the utter nastiness of it, the ivory was from a particularly rare elephant.

Day 3. In the VIP lounge in Gaborone there was a quartet of important local politicians: all sleek and expensively dressed. The most garrulous of them was the woman. She sat opposite the three men and banged on and on about her theories on this, her motives for that . . . and our People . . . from us They rely . . . and we must ensure They have the utmost . . . concern . . . care . . . and of course on the other hand . . . and we mustn't ignore the repercussions of the economic side-effects . . . and the men nodded and smiled and stared at her enormous tits. I fell a-talking to a perky, brown-eyed man who told me he was a salesman in agricultural fertilisers. 'The trouble is,' he said, 'the local way of life has always been "think of the present, never bother about the future": a sort of slash-and-burn mentality. So trying to sell fertiliser which will improve a harvest several months in the future is almost impossible.' In spite of his problems he was remarkably cheerful, but seemed surprised that I was. 'Don't you get bored with all this flying?' he asked.

'There always seems something different to see or hear,' I replied.

'Good,' he said, 'one of the Yiddish proverbs my mother taught me is – "It is important to stay alive, even if it is only out of curiosity".'

Having landed, and being driven from Johannesburg airport back to Pretoria, we were involved in an accident. We were passing a van. Its open back was packed with a large family, 'everyone from granny to the cat'. Three fellows were squeezed in the driving cab. As we were passing there was a terrific bang from their front tyre and the van swerved towards us and rammed us broadside. Our driver hung on to his wheel and we continued in a relatively straight line, but my escort sitting in the back seat turned round to see the van spinning round four or five times before it came to a stop. Luckily it did not roll over, otherwise the whole lot may have been killed.

We hopped out and had a conference, mainly among ourselves; the van people seemed mute with despair or shock. My escort called the police on his mobile telephone and within five minutes we had three tow-trucks beside us. It turned out that we did not need them, as the damage to us was just buckled side-plates [later – total cost £4000] but I had a talk with some of the tow-truck drivers. One lot were computer students and did it for a money-making sideline. They were all illegally latched into the police radio.

'Get much business?' I asked. 'There seems to be a lot of competition.'

'There's enough for us all, there is an average of seventy accidents a day in the Pretoria area.'

When the police arrived and identification papers were demanded it became obvious why the van-load of people looked so glum: they were all illegal immigrants. I had expected the policemen to hector and bully them; I think that they were more frightened by the policemen's chilly politeness.

Day 5.   Today is a day of rest, until I fly back home in the late evening. I am with the Defence Attaché, a brigadier, his brother and their wives. The men are twins and even at their age – fifty-four – are astonishingly similar. The wives are also quite alike, both being attractive and sparky.

We are in a game farm about twenty miles west of Pretoria. It is owned by a friend of the brigadier: V***, a willowy blonde in her thirties. When we arrived she said: 'I cannot resist that face,' and to my surprise, and profound gratification, she took off her large-brimmed hat and kissed me on the mouth.

Her house is built of rocks and poles, there is a wide veranda on two sides, the whole building is covered with a large thatched roof. Within, it is 'Colonial', with animal trophies, 'ethnic' rugs and blockily built furniture. 'A bit Over-the-Top,' V says, 'but the film companies who come here love it.' Her main interest is the preservation of rare species with, as a sideline, the fostering of orphans, mostly elephants and rhinoceroses. All this is very expensive: just one item – the insurance on her rhinos, for example – costs several thousands of pounds. So the film companies who come to shoot safari-type films contribute a good bit of income to pay for all this. Her estate is relatively small, 1500 acres, but large enough to be divided into areas where the big animals can roam without feeling too constricted.

Off we go in a Land-Rover truck, its open back converted into a high-viewing six-seater. We see a variety of herbivores: Burchell's zebra, onyx (now called Honda by the locals, as its face markings resemble the logo on a Honda car), the wildebeest, as South Africans call their gnu, a ridiculous antelope with a long face and a funny little pair of horns perched on the top of its head like a girl's sunglasses pushed up into her hair.

All of us are in khaki-coloured bush kit except for one: 'You're dressed entirely in black,' I remark to V.

'Yes, I have a black hat, black trousers, a black T-shirt, black boots, a pair of black dogs and black servants: my favourite colour.'

We meet a troop of eight part-grown elephants. They come up to chat and take our carrots, which we have brought in the back of the truck. After they have eaten the offerings some of them start to eat the nearby grass, they roll it up into very neat balls before popping it into their mouths. Funny-looking faces, but lovely eyelashes; a trunk is like an enormous caterpillar in texture, shape and in its ability to coil up. I tell V a recipe for eating elephant's trunk which I recently read in the *Daily Telegraph*:

Slice up trunks into disks, as thick as an average steak.
Roast or grill.
Serve with a poached egg in each nostril.

She smiles, inscrutably.

We drive off to see one of V's particular pets, a female rhino. Its name is Thuluai, which means 'lost and found', which she was, being an orphan before she was rescued and sent here. The women's talk gets onto rhinoceros's sexual equipment, then carrots. I overhear one of them saying: 'Oh, I don't know, I could be turned on by a carrot, if it is a nice one.'

We feed the rhino: the black rhino has no teeth, just a long upper lip like a finger, it can push food right down its mouth with this finger in the same way as I had just seen the elephants stuffing grass down their throats. Thuluai's horns are polished and shiny, she rubs them thus against trees: 'Like me with my nails, she's always fiddling with her horns,' V says.

We come upon a couple of cheetahs lounging in the grass. It is extraordinary to be able to walk up to them and squat beside them and stroke them. The one I am stroking starts to purr just like an ordinary domestic Tiddles. I notice that her hindquarters are very similar to those of a hare, with angular upper parts and very long feet and nails that are non-retractable. The cheetah has been domesticated for thousands of years – the Assyrians had them, Cleopatra famously kept them, Akbar, the greatest of the Mogul emperors, had 9000 during his sixty-three-year reign – all captured from the wild, they have rarely bred in captivity – until now. V thinks she has discovered the secret: the female cheetahs need lots of males competing for them to become sexually aroused. She has discovered that that is the same with rhinos, and has suggested that this technique should be tried out with the notoriously low-libidoed pandas.

The lions are in a separate area which only V enters. We watch her playing with them. She kisses one lion on its mouth: a rather dirty mouth, with yellow teeth and blood-stained lips. I hope she hadn't done that earlier this morning, before she kissed me.

Staff Sergeant
Joe Jackson Laughing Thrush III
= * =
Radar Stn. Eu – NE-Sp. #14
Spain

1957 ~ The Costa Brava.   Laughing Thrush III is the only Red Indian I
have ever met. Small and bustling, with a shiny, round, smiling face like
a polished conker, topped by a crew cut, he had a quick, ironic wit and a
filthy mind. He was in charge of an American 'awareness post' near the
village on the Costa Brava where I used to stay. He drank nothing but
Coca-Cola.

He showed me around his 'post' once: what I remember particularly
was the plaque above his desk: it was inscribed with a quote from his
ancestor Chief Thunder Travelling to the Loftier Mountain Heights,
who finally had to admit defeat in his – fully justified – wars against the
white men:

Hear me, my chiefs! I am tired: My heart is sick and sad.
From where the sun now stands I will fight no more forever.

~ *Mr MAYES* ~

Clocks and Watches

Earls Colne

1950s ~ Home.   'Clockie' Mayes had learnt his trade from someone
born in the 1700s. He was one of triplets, all of whom survived, which
must have been a rare occurrence when he was born, around 1860. He
was small and dapper, always in a dark suit and bowler hat: heavy and
thick-linked was the golden chain he draped across his waistcoat, it was
all a-dangle with little keys; fine and golden were the frames of the pair
of pince-nez which he put on his nose to inspect the intricacies of
watch or clock. He had a white moustache and a voice which I can still
hear after fifty years, strangely hoarse and resonant and kindly, like
Father Christmas with flu. Every Saturday he would walk the two miles
from Earls Colne to our house. He then would take out a large, shiny
gold watch from his waistcoat pocket, at the end of the gold chain, and

opening it up he would compare and adjust the time of all the clocks in our house. Having wound them up and set them to rights he would have elevenses in what was known as the 'Servant's Hall' – perhaps a bit presumptuous for a mere farmhouse – then walk back. When he attained his eighty-fifth birthday my father's chauffeur would drive him home.

In his youth he had been a very keen bicyclist, and cycled all round Europe. He brought back a French wife, which shocked the inhabitants of Earls Colne as much as it did when my father did the same sixty years later. I mention him here because his stories of travels abroad helped to create my interest in 'foreign parts', although Mr Mayes's memories of them seemed limited to the distance from one place to another, or to whether the town hall clock was on time and what the food was like. I reckoned him a bit of a hero because he admitted to having eaten snails and frogs. That accounted for his hoarse voice, I supposed.

COLONEL F.R.B. HAWFINCH, CBE

The National Tourist Association
Lusaka
ZAMBIA

1976 ~ Zambia. Happy-go-lucky, a bundle of fun, a laugh a minute, the life and soul of a party, happy as a sandboy, as merry as a mudlark – Colonel Hawfinch is none of these, for by temperament he is an Empire builder, but he was born too late and has had to be an Empire dismantler instead. Tall and burly, with heavy features set in a bulldoggish droop of discontent, he has very bright blue eyes like turquoise beads; a Lancastrian, he pines for his native fogs and drizzles, but as all his money is in Zambia he has to live here.

Courtaulds Ltd has sent me to Zambia to settle a business contract with the government. The Zambians are friendly and cheerful, with a strong sense of hospitality: 'And not bloody surprising,' the colonel says. 'All the cash they are throwing about comes from the World Bank, together with bribes from the Russians to turn communist, and bribes from the Americans and us to stay on our side.' Halfway through our week of negotiations they have invited me to stay for a couple of days in their Kafué National Park, one of the biggest national parks in the world. Colonel Hawfinch has come as general adviser and guide.

My governmental car and driver collect him from his house. A haggard woman with nicotine-stained fingers waves goodbye.

'Your wife?'

'Was. Divorced her. Damned irritating woman.'

'Then why do you still live with her?'

'Might as well. All my friends have left. And what other woman would want me: unhealthy, ageing and a millionaire – in cowry shells and cow pats?'

Off we proceed in the battered Land-Rover.

'The armed incompetent sitting beside the driver is meant to guard us from attack from dangerous animals and terrorists. But he doesn't know his bloody arse from his effing elbow so, if he starts shooting, keep behind him and out of the way of the dangerous end of his rifle. The driver smiles a lot, that's because he's too stupid to understand my comments on his wretched driving.'

The colonel and I are sitting behind, on a makeshift bench built high up above the rear of the vehicle. From that elevated position we have an excellent view of the enormous range and quantity of wild life which inhabits the park – 'and also to keep a look out for the bandits who infest this place. That's why I carry a pistol. Not that it will be much use against a land-mine. I keep it out of sight if possible, the sight of a firearm always *encourage les autres*. Anyhow, it's best not to make enemies and to keep friendly with the terrorists: today's bandit chief is tomorrow's Minister of Defence.'

The following evening: Colonel Hawfinch has suggested that we go out and spot game by the light of our Land-Rover. 'Better than sitting

[40]

in our chalets listening to the termites gnawing.' We set off in the twilight but it has become dark and the lights have been put on. They are a couple of searchlights hand-held by the guard – not the head-lamps, those had been smashed last year when the driver ran into a kudu. As the colonel said: ' "Repair and Maintenance" is an unknown concept in most of the Third World. The whole of this continent is disintegrating into utter, irredeemable disrepair. Can't entirely blame this lot – the salesmen of the Western world unloaded all their rubbishy stuff on to the poor bloody ignorant natives.' The power for our lights comes through two wires, plugged into holes in the dashboard and jammed into position with matchsticks. Many animals which had been nervous and shy during the day seem less wary – perhaps more bemused – in the light of the lamps. The driver takes us prowling around termite mounds or bushes; the guard glimpses the twinkle of a pair of eyes and then fixes the searchlights on them and we see the eyes' owner apparently at peace, staring towards us.

Suddenly there is a multitude of twinkles. We are looking into two thousand pairs of eyes.

'Oh my God, the buffalo. They'll charge us.'

They do. The guard jumps back in his seat with instinctive alarm and jerks the wires out of their holes. We are plunged into darkness. The driver, not to be outdone with fear, stalls the engine. He scrabbles for the starter button.

Hawfinch mutters: '. . . ing, . . . ing incompetent useless buggers. All we can do is pray.'

We are surrounded by the stampede. The noises are loud and varied: intermittent snorts, panting and grunts and the continuous rumble and thunder of 8,000 hoofs. The smell of cattle and dust. The vehicle is shaking and swaying, but there are no noticeable collisions, just a pushing and a rubbing. Hawfinch leans over to me and shouts: 'If the buffalo don't trample us to pulp, the lions that are after them will probably get us. When we get knocked over, try to crawl under the vehicle, I'll see if I can do anything with my pistol.'

Suddenly they are all gone. Silence falls. Everyone breathes out. The guard strikes a match and in its light he manages to reinsert the wires of his lamps into the dashboard and turn them on. He shines them to where the buffalo had gone. For about two appalled seconds we see two thousand pairs of eyes glaring at us again, about to make a return charge. The only difference between that experience and its predecessor is an additional noise, Colonel Hawfinch bellowing 'you . . . ing idiot' to the guard.

We make our way back to the chalets in the dark.

Someone told me that Colonel Hawfinch had died recently. He was cremated and his ashes were scattered in the centre of Manchester. Perhaps he is happy at last, as the old proverb says: 'Happy is the bride the sun shines on, and the corpse the rain rains on.'

Mrs Peter Sawbill

Sunnymede Mansion
Bridgetown
Barbados

1991 ~ Barbados. Mrs Sawbill was one of those people who when arriving at a party would look around to see who was *not* there, so that she could sympathise with them later. If a couple of women were wearing the same hat or dress, Mrs Sawbill was always the first to point it out, with apparent astonishment. I was at a charity 'do' she had organised and overheard her say to a junior member of the High Commission something as follows:

'My dear! How *lovely* to see that dress *again*! Now I wish I hadn't given it to Oxfam! And that *adorable* little hat' – turning to her husband – 'Dear, on the way home, remind me to buy another saucepan.

'And I see Traleen is here, back from school. How's she's grown!

And don't worry about those *amaaazing* spots. Perhaps it's just a symptom of adolescent repression. No, come to think of it, that's the *last* thing Traleen is likely to suffer from.'

1998 March ~ KENYA, Lake Elmenteita

Day 1. An overnight 'red-eye' flight, landing at Nairobi at 10.15 a.m., an hour's drive to the British High Commission; I hand over the diplomatic mail and find a message that I am to spend tonight, tomorrow and tomorrow night at Delamere's Safari Camp by Lake Elmenteita: 16,000 acres of acacia bushland together with the lake; this estate is semi-private, for the Delamere family and their friends and a limited number of tourists.

The Delameres are one of the 'oldest' of the European families to have settled in Kenya. Several of such types were at school with me. Like me, some of them went to Gordonstoun because they were almost completely illiterate. 'You've Rhodesian cousins, have you?' one of them rather snootily said to me. 'Rhodesia is where the Sergeants' Mess emigrated, Kenya is where the Officers' Mess emigrated.'

'Where your family already were, waiting to buy beads?' I asked.

I set off on the ninety-mile journey. I drive fastish, about 80 m.p.h., but still am sometimes overtaken by 'matatus', private mini-buses, crammed with passengers, with such names painted on as 'Secrets', 'Octopussy', 'I Witness', 'Chairlady', 'God's Will', 'Tuff Goin'', 'Shaggy', 'Electric Avenue', 'Askum', 'Tornado'.

The last two miles are along a dirt road. I arrive with a following cloud of dust. It is late in the afternoon. The central reception area is beamed and thatched; there is a veranda; there are bars and stuffed heads and wickerwork chairs. I am led by a servant down a path which meanders between ornamental bushes to my 'tent'. The front part of this is the real 'tent', its small veranda over-eaved with an outer fly cover. Behind the canvas living quarters is a more substantial stone-built washroom and loo area.

Having unpacked and tittivated, I return to the central area to meet the others. There are a dozen of us: Miss Agatha Grimshaw – tiny, stumpy, gnarled, missing a few teeth, grey pigtail, dress seemingly tailored from a length of sacking, swollen feet in 'sensible' and thus painful shoes, lived in Kenya most of her life, famous for her good deeds and charitable kindness; her entourage of a gentle old missionary couple, their son and his wife; a sophisticated American 'opterician' (what's that?) and his wife, both immaculately dressed; two jolly Lancastrians and 'Lollypop', their enchantingly sweet little granddaughter of about five or six; Helmut Heinkel, a businessman from Frankfurt (he seems to think that he and I are some sort of soul-mates, but as I have little knowledge or interest in stocks and shares he may be wrong); and me.

Time for the evening walk: less than a couple of miles, but up three hundred feet to the top of the escarpment which bounds the edge of the lake nearby. We walk along a trail which has been cleared through bushes and under fever trees. There are not many flowers: three of the most conspicuous are the spires of red-hot poker (always full of earwigs in my garden), the flowers and poisonous yellow tomato-like fruit of the Sodom apple (*Solanum incanum*) and a very attractive flower of such a deep purple that it is almost black – 'Hibiscus cannabinus,' the guide says.

The missionaries are sensibly kitted up with boots and rucksacks, the Americans are dapper, I am slightly scruffy. The slope is steepening, the footpath narrowing, I am sweating. Not Miss Grimshaw, she hobbles stoically on with not a word of complaint. Which does not mean she is not talking. She is very knowledgeable. Our guide is a tall, Masai type, who points out the flora and fauna which we pass. She often tells him when she thinks he is mistaken. He is either well mannered or well paid, for he does not lose his temper, just nods gravely.

We have reached the top of the escarpment and are rewarded with the delightful sight of a gang of smiling servants standing behind tables of hewn logs, upon which have been placed bowls of nibbles and glasses of chilled Chablis, a small barbecue to one side wafts the scent of tiny bits of meat; these are skewered and offered with the murmured information of 'Thomson's gazelle'. I am surprised that Miss Know-all has not interrupted, 'No it is not, it is Whetherspoon's Williebeeste'. I sip the wine, gnaw my gazelle (delicious and slightly smoky) and look over the lake. Far off, amid the mountains on the other side, a huge thunderstorm is taking place; lightning sears through the blue-black of the clouds; to the edge of the cloud bank we can see rain, dark veils descending slowly; further to the east light from the setting sun splays out in uneven beams. To our left, but also over the water, an isolated ridge of mountain has a profile not unlike a prone President de Gaulle.

'We call it the Sleeping Warrior,' says the guide.

'You call it the M'Tusi Wingi Wangi McBangi Wallop,' says Miss Know-all.

The lake is typical of a Rift Valley lake in having no outflow and thus building up an intense alkalinity which is too virulent for fish or weeds. However, it is particularly attractive to the lesser and greater flamingos and it has a breeding colony of great white pelicans. The surface is speckled with waterfowl: the pelicans, elegant in black and white, swan-like spoonbills, stilts, Egyptian geese (honking terrifically). Below us, an untidy flock of flamingos suddenly takes off, neatly separates, and forms into long skeins.

'What do you think of this?' Helmut asks.

'Very nice,' I reply.

He smiles indulgently: ' "Nice", in your language, means "exact", or "precise", I expect what you really mean is that it is "pleasing" or "attractive".'

'Yea, probably.'

'And what do you do?'

'I farm for half the time and am a Queen's Messenger for the other half, with a bit of writing in between.'

That smile again, patient: 'There is no room for anything in between two halves. Two fifty per cents make one hundred per cent, and you cannot have more than one hundred per cent, or one whole.'

I feel that he and I are not going to be bosom chums.

He asks me about the future worth of Courtaulds Ltd's shares. I am fairly non-committal: I think he reads more into my ignorance than I intend. [Later – I did not know then that the wretched directors of Courtaulds, having incompetently supervised several years of diminishing profitability, were about to destroy two hundred years of my family name in industrial success by selling out to a Dutch company.]

Day 2. A goodish night's rest in my tent in spite of awakenings by the cries of waterfowl and bushbirds: whistles, grunts, whoops, cooing and tweets.

Reveille at 6.30. I lay in bed for a bit, sipping tea and listening to the gardeners outside, chattering and clucking to each other like hens let out of the coop. I could not unzip the flap of my tent properly so, after struggling with it, I squeezed out of the partly opened aperture on my hands and knees, to find the guide looking at me. 'A bit like being born,' I said, which amused him.

Coffee and tea were laid out in the main assembly hall. Now we are on another walk: through the dew – beaded on spider-webs, pooling in the hollows of leaves, creating a smell of wet earth and seeming to exhale a vast number of flies. Miss Know-all is in front, hobbling frantically to keep up with the loping of the guide; the Lancashire grandparents are lagging right at the back. There is a grumbling cough from a bush, nothing serious, I think, just a bull eland or something, but a little hand slips into mine. It is Lollypop. She does not say anything, just holds my hand: protecting me from lions, I expect.

After a huge breakfast, we all embus into the open backs of two Land-Rover trucks for a safari. We are driven along trails through different 'environments' (as Miss Know-all calls them): groves of fever trees, open bushveld, jungle, a flat grass plain by the lake. Much of the time we can hardly see the overgrown tracks so it feels as if we are gliding through seas of green. There are many birds with good names: laughing dove, speckled mousebird, lilac-breasted roller, rattling cisticola, blue-eared glossy starling, red-cheeked cordon-bleu. The most exciting and beautiful is the rare Narina's trogon, a flitter and shifting of iridescence in the darkness of the jungle – in shape and size very similar to a cuckoo, but with a vividly scarlet breast and belly, the dominant colour on the rest of the bird being a shining, metallic green. The most embarrassing bird is an ostrich. It is a big cock bird, tottering top-heavily on gangly legs, its eyes popping out at us in adoration. It has fallen in love with our car. It follows us, ruffling its wings beguilingly like a fan dancer.

'It's got no fevvers on its legs, they're all bare,' says Lollypop disapprovingly.

'And they're a funny sort of colour, it's got mauve drumsticks,' adds her grandmother.

'The legs of a cock ostrich go purple when it is sexually aroused,' says the guide. 'It cannot sweat; to cool itself, it urinates upon its legs.'

I look at Miss Know-all: for once, she has nothing to add.

The ostrich ends its dance by falling on its knees, its legs splayed out ridiculously behind, shaking its plumes despairingly after our departing car.

Of the animals seen (buffalo, Burchell's zebra, spring hare, hare, baboon, vervet monkey, civet, steenbok, dikdik, eland, impala, Thomson's gazelle, bushbuck and waterbuck) the spring hare is specially attractive. It is not a hare, although about that size, and like a heraldic beast is a conglomeration of other animals: it has a rabbit's face, a donkey's ears, a kangaroo's body and a cow's tail.

It is now late evening, we have had dinner and are out again in the Land-Rovers. The whole of the gloom is a-twinkle with lights, a starscape of shining dots, some gold, some silver, some emerald or ruby or topaz, some sparkling in a galaxy, some shooting past as meteors, others clustering in constellations. The guide can tell us what we are looking at merely by the colour, the distance apart or the movement: most noticeable are the eyes of the spring hares, they bound through the darkness in hoops of light.

Day 3. The others left after breakfast. I said goodbye to them. Helmut and I had a final monologue about stocks and shares. Then, with relief:

Me: 'Well, goodbye then, see you anon, perhaps.'

He: ' "Anon" means "soon". There is no likelihood that we will meet in the near future.'

> ### Ctesse Marie-Alexandra Lanius-Schach
>
> #### 56, Rue Grotte
> #### Paris XVI

1950s ~ Paris.   The countess was one of the several East Europeans my parents used to visit on their journeys to Paris. My mother had been a dancer in the Russian Ballet in Exile, and knew many of the exotic, dramatic, melancholy and often very beautiful pieces of human flotsam from the communist revolution.

When she reached her eightieth birthday the countess decided to commit suicide. She spent the last of her money on gardenias and angel's trumpets. She filled her seedy little Parisian bed-sit with the flowers. Then she wrapped herself up in her sable cloak, drank the last bottle of estate vodka and lay down to be wafted to death in the exotic fumes.

For the remaining five years of her life she earned a living cutting toenails and corns.

> ### Madame Georges Piculet
>
> #### Place Bagatelle, Neuilly sur Seine

1959 ~ Neuilly sur Seine.   I had French relations who lived in a house in Neuilly sur Seine, on the outskirts of Paris. Tante Apollonia, like most of the French, was full of common sense and devoid of surplus sentiment. She had little interest in gardens, and even less interest in paying a gardener wages. She had therefore gathered a large collection of plastic flowers, helped by many friends and relations who were urged to buy a brand of washing powder that was issuing an artificial rose, tulip or daffodil with every packet.

[48]

I had intended, one weekend long ago, to take Tante Apollonia's nubile daughter and wander along the romantic streets of Paris, beneath the budding chestnut trees, pausing occasionally to sit outside a café by a little table, drinking wine and laughing about the passers-by. Instead, I spent most of the time on my knees in the garden, uprooting plastic flowers, washing them in a bucket of soapy water and replanting them. Tante Apollonia, who was working alongside me, sticking in the new flowers with which she had been presented, was learning Chinese at the time. It appears that Chinese has only about ten words, but there are several thousand different ways of pronouncing them. Thus, as I laboured, I heard a strange sequence of noises as my aunt recited her latest vocabulary: 'Chang!', 'Tchang!', 'Ch'ang!', 'Channnng!', 'Chang?', 'Jang!', 'Ch-ang!'

'Tante Apollonia,' I said, to relieve the monotony of the conversation, 'all this gardening reminds me, why don't we go and see Roseraie de l' Hay?'

'I have never heard of it,' Tante Apollonia replied, 'but', she added magnanimously, 'that does not mean that it does not exist. We will look for it on the map of Paris, and then I will drive us there.'

As well as a map I found a book, Graham Stuart Thomas's *Old Shrub Roses*, which mentioned the gardens:

The rose gardens [of Roseraie de l'Hay] are laid out in geometrical designs with a scope and exactitude such as we do not dream of over here. As a general rule the paths are of carefully raked shingle, bordered by grass or box edging. The lines are impeccably correct, the edgings perfect, and the grading of the plants most carefully effected by pruning and training.

. . . The centre piece . . . is a small geometrical pond, surrounded by long beds of decorative shape, containing fine modern roses and also such old Hybrid Perpetuals as 'Frau Karl Druschki' and 'Ulrich Brunner'. As a background there is the great pergola and central arbour, all of which is completely covered with the Wichuraiana variety 'Alexandre Girault'.

. . . on every side above and below are roses – roses short in

[49]

little bushes; roses swinging on ropes between little pillars; standard roses of all heights with solid bushy heads, or weeping from a perfect umbrella top; roses over arches square or rounded. Everywhere are blossoms and scent.

Tante Apollonia's driving was ambulatory. Like her walking it wandered, pausing to inspect things as she proceeded, zigzagging from verge to verge. Sometimes she braked suddenly to peer into a shop window, or she hurried eagerly across a roundabout to scan the headlines of the papers being sold in a stall opposite; a friend would be waved at. Ignoring the curses of a bus driver who thought that she was turning left, she would suddenly dart to the right, wiping across the nose of a bicyclist. I sat frozen with horror as we meandered thus across Paris.

We reached the haven of the car park and entered the garden. It was early June, every flower seemed at its most glorious, the scent was heady. Even Tante Apollonia was impressed, but what she liked best were the names. She seemed to know everybody. '*Mon Dieu*, has *she* had a rose called after *her*?! . . . That old Man! We girls were always told: "Never go up alone in a balloon with Monsieur le Duc." . . . I used to play tennis with this family, always cheating . . . Huh. Imagine! A rose named after *him*! After what he did to his poor mistress . . . My mother always distrusted her, that one, she always had too many buttons on her gloves . . . *Merde alors! Une salle Boche!*'

Suddenly, to my embarrassment, she sprang lightly over one of the little box hedges and, having delved under a bush, produced a stone. It was a perfectly ordinary flint.

'Palaeolithic, of course,' she said, 'Mousterian. A hand axe. It reminds me. I must go to Syria tomorrow to help in deciphering the new Hittite tablets they are excavating at Skaje Guezi.'

'But you can't read Hittite,' I objected.

'*Non. C'est domage.* I will have to learn it during the journey. So you cannot stay here, all alone with my poor innocent daughter. I will send you to our cousin Madame Croixrouge in Bordeaux, she is bored, she is a bit mad: she likes the English.'

> ## OWEN S. GRIFFIN, MBE
>
> ## The United Kingdom Mission
> ## to the United Nations
> ## Dag Hammarskjold Plaza
> ## New York

1999 ~ New York. 'Look! Look at them! Never again in your life will you see such a collection of thugs and bullies.' Thus storms my companion, pointing to the squad of uniformed men marching past to the skirl and thump of their band: that of the Irish detachment of the New York police force. 'They just shot an unarmed street peddler, *forty-one* times they fired at him – forty-one – and out of forty-one bloody shots they missed the poor bugger *twenty-two* times, and for most of that time he was lying dead on the pavement beside them. And they have the bloody impudence to call themselves Celts. They're less Celtic than my wife's Siamese cat. Look at this next lot! The O'Conorvitches, the Paddy O'Finkelsteins, Mike MacBongo from County Congo and here comes a troop of little old Leprechauns from the Balkans via the Bronx.

'Now, look there, this lot, dressed in Scottish tartans and sporrans and they have the impudence to carry a banner saying "British Out!"'

My companion is from our NATO office. He is a Welshman. It is lunch time and we are watching the St Patrick's Day Parade in New York.

I wish he were a bit quieter. We are surrounded by crowds of happy people sporting the shamrock and wearing green.

Owen cheers up: he has some friends from the NATO Dutch contingent near him and they are talking about their Prime Minister, Wim Kok: 'I've heard of people who were neither one thing nor the other, that fellow obviously is both,' he says.

[51]

1998 March ~ The CARIBBEAN

Day 2. As this is one of my last journeys as a Queen's Messenger, I have been allowed to bring Dominie – as long as I pay her fare and other costs. We have checked in at the beach club: large verandaed rooms, lovely gardens which, over the last thirteen years, I have seen develop from their early planting to the jungle-like burgeoning of today, some dining and drinking areas with thatched roofs on poles, a swimming pool for the young, the old or the unadventurous, and a good beach of white coral sand over which coconut palms lean. Some of them are shading us now, as we breakfast on one of the lawns. We can hear the sea and smell its saltiness – just, because the smell of bacon and eggs and toast and coffee is even stronger – and as we eat we can admire the shrubs and trees nearby: hibiscus, frangipani, bougainvillaea, bauhinia, flambeau. One especially beautiful flower is like a Christmas tree ornament hanging from the tip of a long, arching branch. It is a deep pinky-red, the curvaceous petals are finely divided, from the centre of them is suspended a very long stamen, surrounded by a bunch of stigmas, each tipped with a tiny golden puff of pollen. It is *Hibiscus schizopetalus*, also known as the 'dissected' or 'coral' or 'fringed' hibiscus. Some tiny doves potter about the lawn, near our table. Dominie thinks them absolutely sweet until one of them flies into the feathery fronds of the overhead palm. It fidgets about – preen, preen – scratch, scratch – stretch – 'coo, coo – coo, coo – coo, coo' – SPLAT! – Dominie has been shat on.

The dove has deposited an enormous amount of dark red gunge. 'God, that awful bird, a whole pomegranate, plus the pips!' She fusses and mops and wipes herself. As if apologising for their avian cousins, a pair of yellow waistcoated bananaquits come and hop about on our table, with curved beaks they puggle under the lid of the marmalade jar to sip the contents.

We are joined at 9.25, 'five minutes before parade', by the Queen's Messenger's local escort, a resident called Colonel Ian Elgin. He carries a businessman's case; in one compartment there is a row of blue and black pens, printed instructions, a map board and wax pencil, a list of emergency telephone numbers and passes to the High Commission and 'security' areas of the airport. This is the section he will be using tomorrow, when he escorts me to and from my flight. The other side also has a row of pens, but multi-coloured; there are calling cards, an address book, booklets on the flowers, trees, birds and butterflies of Barbados, and maps. This is what he will be using today.

'Today,' he says, 'will be a botanical day because you are both keen gardeners; tomorrow will be a buildings day, George being away at work and having already visited the interesting houses and churches.'

'Barbados,' he continues, 'is the most easterly of the Caribbean islands. Because of this it was usually the first one visited by the slave traders, who would then sail their way along the Windward Islands, the Leeward Islands, past Puerto Rico and Hispaniola, ending up at Jamaica. The best slaves were usually sold first, in Barbados: the strongest, handsomest and most friendly (that, at least, is what a Bajan says when meeting a Jamaican). The island is 166 square miles – about the size of the Isle of Wight. Being of coral rather than volcanic in origin, it is rather dull geologically and contourally, but it is near enough to the plate of the South American continent to have had a few adventures in upheaval and subsidence: there are 'highlands' which include Hackleton's Cliff, an inland escarpment with almost sheer cliffs a thousand feet high, and limestone caves and tunnels which burrow hundreds of feet below the ground; the flora is relatively limited, but there are some interesting indigenous plants unique to the island, and the fauna is augmented by many migratory birds. Historically it is quite interesting in that it is an English, rather than British, colony, the main flood of immigrants being English Royalist refugees escaping from Cromwell's republicans. As the years passed some of these emigrants sank into poverty; they interbred, which did no good to either their bodies or their brains; now the descendants of the gallant English cavaliers and their butlers and grooms have degenerated into "poor whites", "red-legs", "eky bekys" and "buckra Johnnies".'

Having finished his summing up, Ian stuffs us into his car and drives us along narrow streets edged by cosy 'chattel' houses, with verandas and porches and shuttered windows, and along lanes which wind between miles of sugar cane plantations.

'Everything looks very healthy, do these plants have any parasites or vermin?' I ask.

'Typical bureaucratic balls-up: there are cane rats. So they imported mongeese to kill the cane rats, then they discovered that the rats are nocturnal and the mongeese work only in daylight so that they have had to turn their hungry attention to the indigenous animals and birds.'

Our first stop is at a small car park next to some woodland. Ian gets out and points towards the boskiness: 'This is called "The Flower Forest". It took two years to create and was opened in December 1983. It is approximately fifty acres. The height above sea level averages 850 feet, there is a variety of soil and rock types, and it is suitably far from the debilitating influence of the sea winds, thus you will find that a large variety of trees, shrubs and flowers are on view. A round walk has been made through several different types of habitat: forest, orchard, meadow, palm grove, open valley and narrow ravine, semi-formal flower gardens and rockery. This walk is approximately half a mile. I estimate it will take you thirty-five minutes, give or take five minutes. I will leave you as I have to go shopping and will meet you back here at 10.50. The walk has been planned in an anti-clockwise direction; I prefer to go clockwise, myself, it means that I do not get stuck behind ditherers.'

Dominie and I meander through glades and open lawns, under trees and above the flowing of a stream, through a gorge, with cliffs above and caves below. Down some of the cliff faces there are cataracts of roots from bearded fig trees. It is thought that the original discoverers of Barbados, the Portuguese, named the island Los Barbados – the bearded ones – after these trees. Dominie has never been outside Europe before and it is remarkable to her to see 'pot plants' in the wild: to walk under poinsettia trees, to see the glossy leaves of rubber plants thirty feet up the trunk of a forest giant and mother-in-law's-tongue growing as massed arrays of spikes in the shadows, and magnificent stands of orchids at random in the glades.

We are five minutes later than the estimated thirty-five minutes, as we spent too long under a grove of spice trees, looking for nutmegs. We found a handful and show them to Ian. He expounds: 'The nutmeg is an evergreen originating in the islands of Indonesia. The fleshy outer rind conceals the nut, which is encased in a thin shell. This is partly covered by a scarlet mesh which smells and tastes even more strongly than the nut. It is peeled off the shell and dried and sold as "mace". The rind is also useful, being ground up, steamed and squeezed. The juice congeals into "nutmeg butter".'

[54]

'What's that used for?' Dominie asked.
'I have no idea.'

Ian took us on two other plant expeditions: one was to the Andromeda Gardens, positioned on an escarpment overlooking the district of Bathsheba and particularly attractive with boulder gardens, the other was to Codrington College and its grounds of superb woodlands. (The college was built in 1743 as a seminary for the Anglican Church in the West Indies.) However beautiful, what I liked most about many of the plants was their oddness, either their names or their singularity. Among the most appealing names were clammy cherry, scratch wyth, sucking bottle, fiddlewood and screw pine. The most peculiar plants included the sandbox tree, with a spine-covered trunk and an odd seed case which was once used as a sand shaker (before the invention of blotting paper); the soap berry tree, whose black seeds were imported into England to be made into waistcoat buttons; and the indigenous toothpick plant (or macaw palm), whose trunk is a-bristle with long black spines.

On a previous journey here I told Ian that I occasionally collect plants for the Royal Botanic Gardens at Kew. 'Ah,' he said, 'then you may be interested in our extinct tree.'

'?'

'The Bajan mastic tree was related to the mastic tree of South America from which they make chewing gum. It grew only on this island. It was so tall and straight that it was ideal for building – whether ships or houses. By 1856 the last tree had been felled and the plant became extinct – so they thought.

'There is a crack in the ground, a ravine about eighty feet deep, with a bridge over it. A short while ago a botanical friend of mine saw that a tree which had been growing at the bottom of the ravine was now tall enough to have reached the bridge. He plucked some of the leaves. By the look of them he thought it could be a Bajan mastic. But he is now dead and nothing has happened about it.'

Ian took me to the tree and I took cuttings of the glossy-leaved twigs in reach and sent them to Kew. We have not yet heard of their analysis. Perhaps they will have to wait until the cuttings get reasonably large.

Day 3. When I was a youth I was an eager member of a Mountain Rescue team and also an adequately useful wing-three quarter in the rugger field. The reasons for this were that I am alarmed at heights and think sports are boring (to watch, anyhow); similarly, one of the reasons I am a Queen's Messenger is that I have a dread of aeroplanes. It seems to be a perverted quirk in some people to volunteer to do the very things that they want to do least. When I am fully retired I am going to take up billiards, bridge and bungee jumping as my hobbies. Anyway, compared with the 350 ton Jumbo aircraft that brought us to Barbados, the twin-engined Baron Beechcraft 58 that I am in for today's island hop is so small that it seems to rock through the sky at the slightest change of atmospheric pressure. Dominie is somewhere below me, with Ian, setting off for more touring of the island; here I am alone, but for the pilot and co-pilot in the cockpit, and eighteen diplomatic bags and an ice-box of food and drink on the other three seats in the passenger area. I am flying from Barbados to nine other islands, then back to Barbados, involving a total of twenty landings and takings-off, most of which seem to be difficult. I have some books about the islands with me, just in case I can ever afford to take Dominie on another Caribbean holiday.

Up we go, soaring into the void . . .

The nose of the aeroplane dips so there is more of a sensation of flying as I now can see directly ahead with the clouds coming towards us, then gliding overhead. An island sprawls in front, its shaggy hog's back humping up into the clouds, its flanks dappled with patches of cloud-shadow and sunlight and with the contrasting greens of forest and fields: this is Grenada ('pronounced Gren-ay-der. 133 square miles. Volcanic. "The Island of Spice" – famous producer of nutmeg and mace,' my book tells me).

One of the many dials on the dashboard visible past the shoulder of the co-pilot says 2500 feet. We are going alongside the coast now, there are turquoise shallows and little bite-shaped beaches, bungalows with their corrugated-iron roofs painted a dark red and dusty tracks weaving between them, a marina, a pier, the yachts moored alongside like a row of white piglets suckling a sow, the finger of our runway jutting into the sea . . .

Eventually I can see the runway straight ahead; Port Salines landing-strip is beside a small group of buildings. I have a quick exchange of bags with the meeting officer, reboard the aeroplane and off we go again.

We fly over the archipelago of the Grenadines: a sprinkling of rocks, islets and islands, the islands such as a schoolboy would draw with exaggerated curves and indentations to the beaches and bays and isthmuses, all united by swirling patches of colour which range from pale lime green to Cambridge blue to every sort of turquoise and sapphire and navy blue-black; all too beautiful to be real, a dream of some alien unattainable heaven; a most lovely four-masted fully rigged sailing ship, her sails furled at rest, lies in the bay below, and in the pellucid waters closer ashore two motor boats leave curved trails of wake like comets in a morning sky.

The runway of Kingstown is tucked away almost behind a cliff. Just before the runway there is a bay and two rock spurs which stretch out like arms into the sea. It seems as if the little aeroplane has to swerve round the first arm and hop over the second before we swoop down on to the landing-strip.

Someone had not been so lucky. The hull of a Curtis 46 roosts in the sun outside the low buildings: the three tips of its portside propeller curl back like flower petals; it had tilted on landing.

The whole place is percolated with the rich scent of coconuts from a small copra factory beside some palms.

On the shoreline below are 'The Pitons' of St Lucia: extraordinary rocks 2500 feet high, they are pointed, like huge bombs, and are the cores of eroded volcanoes. We're joggling and lurching through a flock of vicious little clouds: 'What happens if this jumping around gets any worse?'

'The wings will fall off, man.'

Now we are approaching the cosy little runway of Castries: to port, the sea; to starboard, houses with verandas and pretty gardens, built amidst a busy, bumpy landscape of hillocks, knolls, mounds and peaklets. Within the gardens coconut and royal palms tower over bananas and flowering plants which include masses of bougainvillaea and the scarlet-topped flambeau tree.

A steel band is pinging and panging quietly at a camera, a few chaps loaf about under the trees that grow between the runway and the sea. They are waiting for the local football team to return from winning some important match. No great excitement – how pleasantly different from the tribal hysteria at home.

As I take off I see someone water-skiing below and feel a wistful twinge.

I can see the great Diamond Rock, which marks the approach to Martinique. Strange, although the island is French, it is the one which looks most like England: small fields with hedges, parkland, large isolated oak-like trees. As the view gets more urban, I notice big roads with white lines, telegraph poles, a city, a brick-making factory on the beach; it is bleeding a horrible rust-red stain into the sea, the water is polluted for several square miles. What a disgusting, scruffy, contaminating animal the human being is.

The meeting officer is a charming, suave Frenchman: a stringy-looking fellow in gym shoes with cavernous, slightly blue cheeks; he is smoking a Gauloise or something equally filthy. He signs for the bags, hands me two others, we chat a bit and he leaves. I have to wait while the pilots pee and buy fags, so I walk over to the sedgy/reedy boundary near the aeroplane. There are some attractive flowers: a small bushy mimosa, a type of daisy, a lilac-coloured bell-bine, a tiny bright blue flower and two species of the pea family, one with yellow flowers, the other scarlet. Damsel flies flit about in the still, hot air, they each have four transparent wings, each wing has a large black spot. There is a beautiful ladybird with a brilliant iridescent silver stripe down its back. A locust disturbed by me flies out from a tussock and is snatched out of the air by a grackle, I feel rather guilty. Some small scarlet birds are in the reeds – cardinals?

As we fly away I see the peak of Mount Pelée shrouded with cloud. This is the volcano which blew up in 1902, killing all but two of the 40,000 inhabitants of St Pierre. Ironically, the two were saved from the fires and poisonous gases by being imprisoned in a subterraneous dungeon.

There are fewer clouds now; a couple of thousand feet below, their blue-black shadows dapple the navy-blue sea. Some of those billows have formed into the typical anvil shape of storm clouds . . . wobble,

wobble, jump, joggle, the wings flipping at their tips like a goose trying to take off. Bloody co-pilot turns round to look at me and grins a vast expanse of merry teeth. I smile weakly back.

A steep cliff rises out of the sea, the foam at its feet is of breaking rollers. We have reached Dominica. The runway, further up the coast, is minute, merely a narrow concrete glade edged with palm groves.

I have a packed lunch and have now started to nibble its drab contents as we fly to the next island: cold meat (very tough beef, tasteless turkey, gristly ham), tinned mixed veg (yuk), very good fruit salad, cheese. The 'Cola' drink tastes of burnt string.

Antigua is flat, with a big central plain, but the shoreline is interesting: curvilinear undulations of beaches, bays, bottle-necked isthmuses, sand banks and lagoons; how pleasant it would be to walk and swim along them all.

After refuelling (we use thirty gallons an hour at 180 m.p.h.) we fly on to Anguilla. Being a coral island, it is flat as a cow-pat: relatively dull to look at from afar, even the vegetation looks scabby from above, like lichen on a tile; but the pleasant Scots girl who met me said the beaches are wonderful.

The next stop is on Beef Island, one of the British Virgins, an archipelago of about forty islands of which the main ones are Tortola, Virgin Gorda, Anegada and Jost Van Dyke, all totalling sixty square miles. Even from up here I can see that tourism concentrates on the 'rich and rare', preferably in large yachts and gin palaces. Amid the speckling of deckle-edged islands and rocks I can see huge boats; they are moored beside lovely beaches, or sailing in a sea all silver and blue and glinting.

My last delivery-cum-collection was at St Kitts. All eighteen bags have been delivered and I have collected fourteen new ones. My return journey to Barbados is a flight of two hours, then the last of twenty takings-off and landings – then dinner with Dominie and Ian. At present, it is late afternoon. The engine of the little aeroplane is emitting a soporific drone. We are all alone in space, flying through the streaky oranges and reds and purple-blacks of a sunset. Islands lie in the waters below, like resting whales. I feel dozy. Perhaps that is why I feel at one with the elements of the air, for it is only when we are asleep that we can really fly.

Josef Ritter von Zawadski

W. Petro

1940s ~ Occupied Europe. Both these men were associates of my father in the Special Operations Executive during the Second World War. All I remember of the first is that he was normally known as 'Polish Joe'. He used to come to Colne Engaine in a variety of uniforms. One of them is still hanging in the 'no-use-anymore-but-don't-want-to-throw-away' cupboard, together with my father's court dress in velvet and cut steel, Dominie's wedding dress, my great-great-grandfather's swallow-tailed hunting coat, covered with splashes of Essex clay a hundred and fifty years old, and my battle dress (which never saw a battle) and university gown (which did).

Petro was a white Russian. He was small with beady dark eyes and black hair brushed down so flat it seemed to have been enamelled on his head. He was just known as 'Petro'. No-one knew what the 'W' was, even after he had written his autobiography, *Triple Commission*, published in 1968. It was called that because he was awarded a commission in all three services: the army, navy and the air force. He described himself as 'linguist, balletomane, art collector', but he was much more than that. During his extraordinary life he had been an Artillery officer in the czar's army, served in the French army as Liaison Officer to the communists in Siberia, commanded Romanian troops, went gold-mining in Mongolia, advised the Warlord of the Yellow River on irrigation and warfare and served as a British officer in the Punjab Regiment in Hong Kong. He ended the war in SOE.

He is dead now, and our house is still guarded by the Tang Dynasty tomb attendant that he gave my parents.

The spies, saboteurs and others of that ilk had many cards, to remind themselves who they were. My father had four. The one I prize most is:

```
INTER-SERVICES
RESEARCH
BUREAU

Name:       George Courtauld
Rank:       Captain
Serial no:  0001
```

Beat that, 007!

```
Colonel Richard Sparrow
The Lodge
Colne Engaine
```

1880–1960 ~ The British Empire.   'Dick' Sparrow was a cousin of mine: a soldier and traveller. It was remarkable how much he resembled Colonel Blimp: the muscular but podgy body, the bullet head, the white walrus moustache, the tiny, pale, shrewd eyes; patriotic, brave, loyal, utterly trustworthy. In spite of his shape he was a highly skilled sportsman – whether on a horse, or on foot, or on hands and knees, with a gun, or a lance, or a rod. His house was a charnel of dead animals: he put his umbrella in an elephant's hollowed-out leg, hung his hat on a red deer's antlers and, standing on a scatterment of carnivore skins, would fill his pipe from a rhinoceros horn under the reproachful, glassy stare of kudu, moose, boar, bear and tunny fish; his famous egg collection consisted of eggs, the nests from whence they came, and the stuffed hens, like tea-cosies, placed on top.

[61]

He would read the lesson in church faultlessly and beautifully; the New Testament bored him rather, but the Old Testament was intoned with impressive sonority, the names of Mesopotamia, Babylonia and Palestine enunciated with the authority of one who had been to them all.

He was convivial and made friends easily, although his patronising affection for the denizens of the Empire would nowadays be thought infuriating. People were rude to him only once, as his reply was more crushing than any witty repartee or stern retort: a cold, arrogant stare of disgust. He thought himself a born superior. As a small boy I, too, felt he deserved my admiration, which is more than can be said for many people I meet today, cleverer, better educated, less naive and more painstakingly tactful though they be.

1998 April ~ CHINA, Hong Kong

Day 3. In Hong Kong the Queen's Messengers are honorary members of the Missions to Seamen, an Anglican missionary society. Last time I was here I asked the padre in charge if I could go with him on one of his tours of inspection. So today I am.

The society was founded in Cardiff in 1856. Now, in two hundred of the world's largest ports, it provides services for the spirit, the body and the brain. Use of these services is offered to any professional seafarer, whatever his religious denomination. The local clubs include chapels, restaurants, bars, libraries and sleeping accommodation. Although an Anglican institution, the mission was joined here by the Catholic Apostleship of the Sea and the Lutheran Danish Seamen's Church. The overall manager is the Revd Peter Ellis, who is Welsh and burly. In black from head to toe except for the white of a dog collar and the brown ends of two cigars sticking out of the breast pocket of his shirt, he has balding, grey hair and fluffy side whiskers. He hates the sea, hates sailing, likes people; has visited almost seventy thousand ships in the six years he's been padre here.

I was picked up by his launch early this morning. *The Flying Angel* is forty-five foot overall with a bridge forward, a main saloon with centre table and benches and a brass crucifix on a wall and shelves of books and leaflets. There is a crew of two Chinese, dressed nattily in whites: shorts and shirts. Ban is the coxswain and Ctn (so it sounded), the engineer.

We have arrived at the container port of Kwai Chung, a huge complex which handles over fourteen million containers a year. We walk past the world's biggest warehouse (9,000,000 square metres – more than two square miles); alongside lines of cranes, I count the wheels on one – eighty-six of them.

The Zim Euroism is being unloaded. She is Jewish owned and crewed. The officer who is showing us round looks like an Indian film star (without the damp eyes and podgy features) and he was born in Bombay, but he is Jewish and his name is Michael Solomon. All is shipshape and Bristol-fashioned, and so it should be: the ship is on her maiden voyage. She is huge: 352 metres long by 32 metres wide. The bridge is packed with ranks of computer screens. On one, we can see the weight of each container upon the ship's structure, from port to starboard, from stem to stern. The ship can sail from, say, A to Z, via M and O, all by pre-set computer: theoretically, they tell the computer where they want to go, and then they can go to bed for the duration of the voyage. Should they want to steer this ship manually, it is not with a magnificent spoked wheel of brass and wood, but a teeny twiddle lever no more than four inches high.

Peter hands out leaflets and reminds members of the crew of the facilities available in the Missions' two clubs in Hong Kong. He knows many of the crew. One of them is a superb woman with a shock of frizzy blonde hair and an enormous toothy smile framed in cherry-coloured lipstick. She wears a denim suit, tight as a drumskin, which emphasises excellent legs and the cleavage of a prima donna. She is bubbling with *joie de vivre* and personality. Whilst the captain and Peter are engrossed in conversation in the captain's cabin I secretly look her up on the crew register – Ester Amai, born in Casablanca on New Year's Day 1938: not my idea of an old-age pensioner.

In the launch again: we glide past silent hulks like sleeping whales, past semi-submerged, snouted prows, under the flared-out jaws of bows and rounded bottoms of sterns, between buoys which bob up and down like monstrous seals on the lookout.

[63]

A Muslim ship, this time: the *Al-Sabayia* of Kuwait. The officers look bearded and fierce, but are friendly. 'It must be as steady as a rock, a ship this size,' I say to one of them.

'Not at all,' he replied, 'she is round-bottomed, and as you English say, "she'd roll on damp grass". In one storm she rolled thirty degrees to either side, it was like being on the end of a windscreen wiper.' They have had a difficult journey, getting stuck in the Panama Canal which has shallowed five feet because of the El Niño effect.

Now the *Katerina*: built in Rostok, refitted in Potsdam, registered in Limassol, crewed by Hindus and lying at anchor waiting to be sold. She is rusting and forlorn, old and unloved, her only suitor may be a scrap-merchant – and even then he'll only want her for her screws. We clatter through rusting corridors; the open doors of cabins release musty smells, everything is clammy, paintwork is swelling in tumour-like blisters. We have lunch in the captain's cabin: Peter and I, a mutton curry; the captain, being a vegetarian, fried rabbit food. We talk of revolting food, which is perhaps rather tactless. I recently tried fried cockroaches – crunchy: all legs, wings and feelers. The other day Queen's Messenger Major James S*** told me that he had eaten a sheep's head: he could stomach the brains and tongue and lips and ears and even eyes, but not the gums, they were so tough and rubbery. The padre said that after six years in the South China Seas he could eat most food, but not chicken's feet, all those sinews and toenails. An even more repellent dish was described to me by Peter W***, our defence attaché in the Philippines, where he came across something called 'balut': a duck's egg, just as it is about to hatch, is taken and boiled. It is then shelled and the duckling eaten; interesting are the different tastes and textures of legs and claws and beak and brains and skull and feathers and innards.

It is late afternoon. I point out that we have not yet been on a Christian ship. Peter says no matter, God made all men, and in his inscrutable way accepts the many ways of praising and thanking him. He says Christian sects in China are merging; it is only some of the

older Italian Roman Catholic priests who are resisting any interdenom-
inational co-operation. The other Christian sects are even building up a
rapport with Muslims and Buddhists. There are three million 'open'
Chinese Christians with official approval, but maybe thirty million
'underground' Christians, who do not get approval and are persecuted.

On my way back I thought I had come upon a street party: groups of
people smiling and chattering and gossiping, a noodle seller doing a
brisk trade from his cart, children being hurried along to join the fun,
pickpockets, prostitutes, peddlers and pederasts weaving and fingering
through the crowd. It turned out that a potential suicide was dithering
undecidedly in the scaffolding high above the street. In spite of much
encouragement, he baulked at the jump, so after a bit I carried on to see
if I could get into the night-club Felix, on the top floor of the Peninsula
Hotel. In the men's lavatory there the urinal is backed by a sheet of
plate glass so that you have the impression of peeing one hundred feet
above the roofs of Kowloon, on the heads of the populace hurrying
below. I was told that this gives one a feeling of great power. But it was
shut – too early.

Julius van der Scoter

S.A. M of D – A/s
Pretoria
Republiek van Suid-Afrika

1993 ~ Pretoria.   There is a limpet in this zoo: not in the aquarium – but
hanging on to my arm. I became aware of it a couple of minutes ago
when I was writing down a description of a hamadryad monkey. A
voice, in honeyed tones, said: 'I've been watching you.'

The limpet is tall and angular, a sheep-like, semi-smiling face with
worry creases on its forehead and balding blond hair cut very short. It is
dressed in a pale blue denim suit, with a teeny rucksack in the same
denim held over one shoulder by a well-manicured finger.

'Writing, writing, always writing,' it continued.

'Some people carry cameras about, I prefer to take a notebook.'

'Must be *dreadfully* tiring for your fingers.'

'Not really, used to it.' (Scribble, scribble, scribble.)

'Tourist, are you? All by yourself?'

'Not exactly. Gosh look at the time, I must go and see the lions being fed. Do you know where they are?'

'I'll take you if you want.'

Help! He's got hold of my elbow.

'No, no, no, please don't bother. I don't want to be inconvenient.'

He's still hanging on, he's got a grip like a vice, I hate being touched by total strangers, this is really weird . . . Thank God, here's the lion's cage.

We stare at the lion. The lion glances briefly at us, curls a lip, lifts an eyebrow, sucks a tooth, then continues to gaze into the distance.

The Limpet is excited: 'Look! It has got a little name plate, it has got a name! Ahh! Its name is Maurice! What a *lovely* name! But I do not know *your* name, and you do not know *mine*. I am Julius.'

Five hours later, at a reception at the British High Commission, I am talking to a female owner of a Stellenbosch vineyard. From behind, I hear the unmistakable whine of that Voice: 'Long time, no see.' The Limpet, in a pin-striped suit. He produces his card. It indicates that he is a buyer for the South African Ministry of Defence. He specialises in artillery.

Thomas T. Titmouse

COURTAULDS LTD

Northern Spinning Division
Arrow Mill
Rochdale

1962 ~ Lancashire.   Tiny and fierce, Titmouse kept pigeons and took snuff, which turned his nostrils into little black caves and made him smell as exotic as a spice isle. He had been an aimer in a bomber during the Second World War. When I knew him he was the foreman of a spinning mill where I was learning the trade. He had strong ideas on travel: ' "abroad" is where you go to kill people,' he said.

'So where are you going on Wakes Week?' I asked him.

'I'm not going where everyone else is. Every spinner and weaver and dyer in Lancashire goes off to Spain, to the Costa-bloody-fortune. Their hotels are only half built, with no running water and blocked-up toilets and a view of the back of the bus station. They get sneered at by the waiters, who then interfere with their wives and daughters. Every day they have to fight off packs of Jerries to get a place on the beach, which is covered with broken glass, fag ends and freddies. The water is full of garlic-scented unmentionables floating in oil-slicks of hair ointment and suntan liniments. The food is also swimming in oil and is full of strange things like octopuses and snails and suchlike and it gives them gyppy tummy, and there's not a decent cup of tea for two thousand miles. The weather makes them sweat and come out in heat rashes.

'I think that if home isn't the best place in the world then you're mismanaging your affairs. During the holiday Lady-wife and I stay at home. The streets are empty, there's no queuing in the shops or at the Odeum or having to buy rounds of drinks in the Cotton Comber for people you hardly know. We hire a couple, Ethel and Sidney: she cooks and cleans, he does the garden and the driving. Lady-wife and I sit on the patio in the morning. Ethel comes out with the breakfast – pot of tea, fried eggs, gammon of ham and pineapple and all the trimmings. Then she goes off to make the bed and do the dusting. And I say to Sidney: "Sid," I say, "after you've brought in the coal and washed the car and weeded the front roses, take the wife to her shopping, will you? Then this evening we may go to Blackpool to see the sights or maybe to Harry Ramsden's over in Yorkshire and have a real nosh up."

'By the end of it all Lady-wife and I have spent a tenth of the sum of

[67]

the other poor buggers who are coming home – to find squatters have moved in while they've been away.'

Eliot M.C.R. Woodcock
Rare & Fine Books, Maps, Manuscripts
The Old Floss
Lavenham
Suffolk

1999 ~ Singapore to London flight. Still ten hours to go; I've had lunch, finished the crossword puzzle, got bored with my book, have fidgets in my feet. While tidying up the unoccupied seat next to me, where I have thrown all my dross, I catch sight of the wine list. I always like reading these, for their rodomontadial waffling.

'Structure and elegance enhanced by a pale straw colour and persistent bubbles': this is the champagne (Charles Heidsieck, 1990), very descriptive of the attractive, middle-aged blonde in the row adjacent. And her pretty but slightly petulant adolescent daughter is the hock (Graacher Himmelreich Riesling Spatlese 1997 Romerhof Weinkellerei): 'still young from an excellent vintage, has a pale silvery colour and a fresh bouquet reminiscent of white peaches. Its fine ripe fruit leaves a touch of sweetness and a tingle of acidity.'

Wine list in hand, I wander around the aeroplane to see if I can match more of the descriptions.

Here is a jolly, well-fed old boy, chatting up the stewardesses in their cubby hole: he resembles Peter Ustinov and is definitely the chardonnay (Montagny Premier Cru 1996 Labouré-Roi): 'aged in oak barrels, adding a honeyed nuttiness to its natural ripeness and vivacity.'

In the Business Class a larger, older man, asleep in his seat with his hands clasped over his tummy, is the chianti (Nipozzano Chianti Rúfina Riserva 1995): 'showing off its deep ruby colour with intense red fruits on the nose, well-rounded flavours and a firm finish.'

Another chianti (Classico Doc Riserva 1995 Castellani) is a smart woman ordering a cold towel: 'full bodied and dry, affords a complex final touch of ripe warm fruit with a hint of spice.'

Now, here is the claret (Les Brulieres De Beychevelle 1996), in the Economy Class, a merry chap in tweeds – which must have been terribly hot in Singapore: 'a deep carmine colour, aromas of small red berry fruits.'

Finally: 'smooth and mellow', the port (Taylor's Late Bottled Vintage 1992). That's me.

On my return I meet up with the Chardonnay, now even jollier, and the stewardesses all a-giggle. He turns out to be a seller of rare books, and has given me his card.

1998 April ~ AUSTRIA, Vienna

Day 1. So here it is: after twelve and a half years, over three million miles of travel, I am about to begin my last journey as a Queen's Messenger. It is six o'clock in the morning, I am in my office. I have collected my special passport, my tickets, my waybill and the itinerary. This is typical of a Vienna-based run, ten aeroplanes in four days: London – Vienna – Belgrade – Vienna; Vienna – Zagreb – Vienna; Vienna – Riga – Vienna; Vienna – Kiev – Vienna – London. My car and driver are in the courtyard. We must load up with the dipmail and then set off for Heathrow and Central Europe.

Day 2. I have a few hours this morning before I report for duty at the embassy so have decided to go to the Augarten Park and examine the flakturms, which my guide book describes as 'huge and terrifying'. These concrete towers are two hundred feet high with walls about twenty-four feet thick. There are six of them, built in 1942, in strategic points of defence around the city. Their basic end-use was as anti-aircraft gun platforms with the additional ability of each being able to house up to 30,000 troops – or, more often, people sheltering from air-raids. They are so massive that any attempt to blow them up would also eliminate all the surroundings so, instead, the Viennese ignore them. They are rarely mentioned in guide books; they are omitted from maps; they are not itemised in tourist brochures; there are not even any jokes about them; they do not exist – they are the equivalent of the spinach on a hostess's tooth, the orator's pocket-billiards, the dentist's undone flies.

Two of them are in the Augarten Park. The park was planted in the late seventeenth century in a formal, geometric layout of hedges and avenues and areas of lawn. Much of the avenuing is of pleached lime or chestnut. As I stroll down one of the green alleyways and turn a corner I suddenly see a flakturm looming vastly at the end of the path, like some giant lying in wait. As I approach it rears out of the surrounding foliage and becomes more and more menacing. It is tubular. Near the top it is ringed by a walkway, from which platforms jut out, presumably to take the guns; here and there gun slits or openings are visible, but mostly the walls are blank and sheer, the only marking being streaks and patches of age. I have to tilt my head right back to look under the platforms: strange, no sign of nests of swallow or martin, utterly deserted. It is unlike any other construction I have ever seen, for although it is merely a hunk of concrete, it seems to be alive, radiating repressed malevolence . . . waiting.

There is a rustling in the bushes beside me and I get a hell of a fright: the small man who emerges is dressed entirely in green, from his pointed, round hat to his cape and shorts. For a moment I truly believe I am looking at some sort of Teutonic leprechaun. He finishes buttoning up himself, returns my stare with an indignant scowl, and toddles up the track.

I walk the half mile to the other tower. This one is angular rather than round in cross-section: it is almost Mesopotamian in its elegant and geometrical simplicity, the rectangles of the block house on top, the soaring planes of its construction; it could be a tower of Babel or the tomb of a King of Nineveh.

On 13 April 1945 Vienna had a relatively docile takeover by the Russians. I cannot find out if the flakturms were the centres of any resistance during the war – by the unscarred appearance of these, probably not.

[Later: Queen's Messenger Major Michael S*** sent me a note saying that he had toured a flakturm which had been opened to the public: 'Apparently, of the towers, three are derelict and unused, one is used by the army, one is used as a storage depot by the City Council and one, in Esterházypark, is the only one to which the public has access – and then only limited access. Two of the exterior walls are festooned with climbing ropes and dotted with toe- and hand-holds. Inside, the bottom four floors contain an aquarium, also displays of fish and spiders. Written on the wall at the top of the flakturm in large letters are the words "Zerschmettert in stucke (Im frieden der nacht)', i.e.: 'Smashed to pieces (In the still of the night)."']

There was a period when I hated opening *Country Life* magazine and seeing the advertisements of houses for sale: all one's friends seemed to be selling out, some of them leaving houses which had been lived in by the same family for many generations. Lloyd's was far more effective in destroying the squirearchy than even forty years of malevolence from the Labour party. Similarly, I don't like seeing portraits for sale: it means someone's love, or vanity, or official achievement is no longer of any account. I realised that the ethos of Courtaulds Ltd had changed when the portrait of Samuel Courtauld was moved from its position of eminence in the board room. Today I have come to the Dorotheum, the Viennese auction house, and there is one portrait which fascinates me. I keep returning from the different showrooms to look at it. It is a slightly larger than life portrait of a woman. She is sitting, her body one third turned away from the viewer, but with her head full-faced. She wears a dark, short-sleeved dress, bracelets, rings, three strings of pearl necklaces and drop pearl earrings. Her hair is dark and wavy, cut shortish. It is a lovely face: elegant, serene, aloof, but also voluptuous with deep, dark eyes; maybe Jewish. The picture is in dreadful condition: flaking and cracked, the ornate frame dark with dirt and missing bits of carving. It must have been locked away in some attic of a large house for years, sleeping through pogroms and wars and riots, perhaps the annihilation of the family, finally to be dug out of her East European home and displayed for sale. The label beside it says:

KRAUSZ WILHELM VICTOR (Neutra 1878–1959)
Baden bei Wien   SITZENDE DAME ~ 1901

No-one even knows her name.

Now I am in the town centre, sitting outside one of the coffee houses. There are about six hundred and fifty cafés in Vienna, about one hundred of which can be defined as proper 'Coffee Houses'. These establishments serve the same function as a pub in England or an old-fashioned café-bistro in Paris: somewhere to meet friends, drink one's favourite drink, maybe have a light meal, or just sit and read a newspaper. There is no harassment to drink and go, once you have been served you are free to occupy your seat as long as you like. Like the London chocolate houses of the seventeenth and eighteenth centuries, the speciality of the Viennese cafés is non-alcoholic, but not exclusively so. The London equivalents transformed into private clubs; in Vienna they are still part of the public scene. They are all traditional brass and velvet and marble indoors but if possible I prefer to sit outside and watch people walking past.

'Coffee please,' I'd asked the waiter. He reacted as if I was a customer in a greengrocer's who had asked for 'a vegetable please'. After going through his list of twenty options, I have chosen a Pharisaer: 'strong black coffee with whipped cream on top, served with a small glass of rum'.

It normally contents me to sit and sip and watch the world go by, but there are not many people about in this quiet backwater: so far I have noticed only an old couple, followed by a woman leading a little dog in a red waistcoat. It seems to do nothing but sniff and pee. What is the point of it? What was God's intention? Why does the woman like it? It is little more than a mobile bladder.

Day 3.   Here I am in the FCO once more, but never again: I will be sixty years old the day after tomorrow, officially an old man, too old to work – no longer any use: by decree senile, feeble, ga-ga, doddery, decaying, dribbly and incontinent. Check in my final load of safely delivered diplomatic bags; I must have carried over two hundred tons of dipmail over the last dozen years. Say a fond goodbye to my driver: a nice lot, safe, considerate, and often interesting companions during the 25,000 miles they have driven me to and from airports. Along the main corridor, down the stairs, along more corridors lined with cables and pipes and tubing; sometimes a hiss and rumble will indicate that a hydraulically driven message is winging its way from the House of Commons to 10 Downing Street next door: pressurised air moving hot air for another Queen's Messenger to carry. Into the spartan but cluttered office, by no means home, but it has a friendly familiarity. Unlock my locker for the last time. There is a note in it: official. A goodbye? Some technical details about my old-age pension? A reminder to hand over my passes and passports? An advertisement for zimmer frames or false teeth? No.

'We have not yet got your replacement. Do you mind staying on for a bit longer?'

Incompetent fools. Well, they'll have to wait. I'm too busy being retired for the next two months.

Mr KAUAI O-O
~ O-O IMPORT-EXPORTS ~

Suva
Viti Levu
Fiji

1995 ~ Hong Kong. Mr O-O is enormous, glossy and brown; his face is as round as a bun, with rows of teeth strong enough to crack a human thigh bone. We met at a dinner party in Hong Kong. He said: 'I am a rare item, a busy Fijian. The trouble is that we Fijians live in the Isles of Paradise and until recently never had to work hard for food and clothing. Then you British came along and wanted to make money out of growing sugar and rice, and we islanders said, "Why should we do anything as boring as digging holes and planting and weeding and chopping and harvesting?" so you brought in Indians, all peasants by nature, and they all quietly worked away and looked away and smiled to themselves when spoken to and resented and planned – and bred and bred and bred. Now we Fijians are outnumbered, and you British said, "Well, bad luck, chaps, from now on you'll have to take orders from the coolies, there's more of them than you, that's only fair, isn't it? Cricket and all that." And when we rebelled at the thought, and declared sovereignty in our own land, you forgot who are the people to whom you owe responsibility, to whom you made promises when you took over from our King Thakombau in 1874, and you betrayed us.'

All the while he was saying this his eyes were twinkling and his teeth were gleaming. In spite of his joviality I felt a bit uneasy. People like him once ate people like me.

I told him that a cousin of mine had married a Fijian around 1800, but as I had forgotten both his name and his wife's it could not have been that interesting for him. I later found out that she was called Princess LoKanika, her father being King LatuNanu. My cousin's name was Thompson – bit of a come-down, that – and he was shipwrecked on the island of Naikina.

```
Dame Constance Fantail    D.C.V.O.

        H. M. YACHT BRITANNIA
```

1986 ~ The Pearl River, Canton. 'Blessed are the meek: for they shall inherit the earth.'

Maybe. I have never admired the meek, there's something creepy about them. They have chips on their shoulders and start wars. They write anonymous letters. They point and whisper. After they have blown their noses they inspect the contents of their handkerchiefs. They dislike church bells and the crowing of cocks – which they call 'cockerels'. Being nervous, they wet their beds; then they leave their mattresses in field entrances. They tell long jokes in low voices. Their hands are soft and damp.

The proud often have something to be proud about. Although they can be frightfully annoying, at least they don't go round making trouble by having to assert themselves. When I was a child everyone was proud to be British. Now we are ruled by meek people who see no reason to be proud, so they destroy anything which made us different from other people. The *Britannia* is an example. As islanders we took pride in our seafaring traditions and this pride was personified by the Royal Ship. Her Majesty's Yacht *Britannia* has been 'binned', to be scrapped or turned into an amusement arcade.

Whenever Her Majesty was abroad on the *Britannia*, a Queen's Messenger would come aboard with 'the post', both personal messages and letters for the Royal Family and entourage, and the official stuff for the accompanying staff and politicians. I have been aboard the yacht in two capacities, once as a guest, once as a Queen's Messenger.

I was a guest in the mid-1970s, in the Persian Gulf, when I was starting up business for Courtaulds with the newly rich Arab states. The commercial department of the British Embassy in Bahrain said I could have any Arab guest aboard the *Britannia* who had spent or would spend over £2,000,000 on orders. I reckon it was because of the *Britannia* that I won nearly £5,000,000 worth of business in three months. An additional task was to help Colonel Hardy Amies, the Queen's dressmaker, by briefing his team on the types of textile and dress design most suitable (the basic theme was that Her Majesty had been made an 'honorary man' for her tour of Arabia, thus any evidence that she is female – bosom, neck and shoulders, thighs, waist and hips etc. should be camouflaged). Hardy Amies had been in SOE in the war, and had done things which would have astonished those who think of him merely as a designer of frocks.

In my official capacity, I flew to Hong Kong on 15 October 1986, then took a train to Canton (Guangzhou), where I was to deliver bags to the Private Secretary to the Queen, on HMY *Britannia*. There were two bags, a personal one for Her Majesty – small, holding only a couple of letters – and a large one to be delivered to HMS *York*, the escorting ship.

The three-hour train journey was interesting enough: the carriage furnished in rows like a bus, the scenery outside showing south China at harvest; a television screen above the communicating door depicting scenes of ecstatically happy textile workers busy spinning, warping and weaving on frames, creels and looms – remarkably inefficient and antiquated.

In Canton my escort and I were put up in one of the best hotels in China: the White Swan. Almost a whole wall of my bedroom was one huge windowpane. It overlooked a bend in the Pearl River, as busy with ferries and sampans and junks as the Kowloon–Hong Kong channel. I slept with the two bags shackled to the down-pipe of my bedroom radiator. In the morning I boarded a mini-bus for the forty-mile drive to the meeting place. Other passengers included some senior sailors, immaculate in their whites. On the front of the bus was a large sign which said 'VIPS MAKE WAY'. As this was written in English, almost no-one could understand it. It was harvest time, so the narrow roads were teeming with farm traffic: tumbrels, waggons, women tottering under the weight of yokes, men zigzagging on overloaded bicycles – all these had to be dodged. When we reached the meeting point I was put on a white cross painted on the jetty's edge. There I waited for half an hour. Then a little black dot appeared downstream – the *Britannia*. Behind her was a little grey dot, HMS *York*. To one side was a crescent of larger shapes, each venting off billows of yellow smoke: the escort of coal-fired battleships of the Chinese navy. The whole Armada sailed past, halted in mid-stream, swung round and edged towards us. The *Britannia* gangway came down exactly to my feet. A superb bit of seamanship. I climbed up the gangway, was piped aboard, took off my hat to pay homage to the quarter-deck, and handed over the Royal bag.

My family having been silversmiths for a hundred years, I cannot resist a hallmark, but when inspecting the cutlery in the *Britannia*'s galley, I gave an involuntary exclamation of surprise: 'EPNS!'.

'Yes,' replied Dame Constance, who had wandered in, looking elegant and a bit vague. 'We had to give up having proper silver years ago. Everyone pinches it. Even the Heads of State. Pretty well every Presidential palace in the world has a spoon or ashtray with HMY *Britannia* engraved upon it.'

That night 100,000 schoolchildren danced on the jetty. The Queen appeared serene and interested and polite at every moment, although the National Anthem was played scores of times, on instruments that seemed to range from Mongolian nose flutes to paper and comb: I'm surprised she hasn't gone stark raving bonkers, being followed about everywhere with that most dreary of dreary tunes.

Cyril G. Finfoot

New Deal Treks
Kathmandu
Nepal

1985 ~ Kathmandu. This man came into a bar, offered drinks all round, looked for his wallet and exclaimed: 'My God! Someone's pocked my picket!' Having borrowed money from some of us, he left his card. We never saw him again, of course.

Zara Sapsucker

Orient Bizarre

23 Dogboilers Road
Hong Kong

1990 ~ Hong Kong. This American antique dealer specialised in oriental pornography: Japanese pillow books, Indian and Cambodian erotic temple wall carvings, rudely active little Chinese people carved from ivory, beautifully bound travel journals of European lechers, assorted 'aids': instruments and body parts and God-knows-whats in jade and gold and ivory and rosewood. I thought it macabre that such a dear little old lady would talk about them with such knowledge and enthusiasm.

1998 July ~ THE PERSIAN GULF

Day 1. My return to the office after two and a half months. No change. Someone has been scoffing in the loo. It has enraged Higher Authority which has pinned a notice to the door:

It has been brought to the attention of Management
that personnel have been partaking of comestibles
within the confines of these ablutions.
This practice must cease
forthwith.

Another piffling notice is among the newspaper cuttings in the 'Points of Interest' book: a declaration from our new rulers that they disapprove of Old Etonians being in the Diplomatic Corps, and will oust them.

Day 2. Having arrived in Bahrain yesterday evening, I now have two days of fairly intensive work, delivering diplomatic bags to five different countries, returning back here between journeys. My transport is a privately chartered aeroplane, a Fairchild Metro III. It has two Garrett turbo-prop engines, can carry a load of 16,000 lb., is the same length as a canal longboat, and inside it has a cockpit which holds the pilot and co-pilot; the remainder of the interior – rather scuffed and battered – is mainly cargo space. There are three bucket seats: one for me; one for my American equivalent; and one for our escort. The air-conditioning does not work until the engines have been started up, and it can get like a furnace inside.

This Queen's Messenger journey is always one of nostalgia to me, a reminder of the 1970s when I was a businessman drumming up trade for a department I had started up in Courtaulds, 'turn-key' furnishing the new buildings which were sprouting out of the sand like concrete mushrooms nourished by the flow of oil: hospitals, hotels, palaces, whole new townships. I could offer everything from initial design and specification to the installation of fittings and furniture and the total supply of all equipment.

Today, Mitch, my American counterpart, is large and cheerful and has an unfortunate tendency to find many things amusing – unfortunate, for his laughter causes him to sweat and the temperature here is already above 40° C. Katie, our escort, is a woman petty-officer from the American navy: taciturn, wiry, with a jutting jaw; her main job is to sit on the bags in the aeroplane when Mitch and I need to leave them to have a pee.

We took off half an hour ago. Mitch is already asleep, Katie is reading a magazine (on wrestling or body-building, I suspect), I am reading the June edition of *Antiquity* and have just come across the longest word I have ever read in non-pretentious writing: 'biogeochemicogeomorpho-logicogeological'. I suppose I could work out what it means if I bothered. But I'm not going to, the muggy heat and smell of hot engines and the vibration and the continuous roar of the propellers are mind-numbing.

We land at Riyadh. The temperature is 44° C. The sunlight bounces its glare and heat off the tarmac outside the Private Arrivals building. I hand my diplomatic bags to the receiving officer. He is having an argument with a gang of officials.

'I gather that you've got over half a ton of bags for me,' I say gloomily.

He is even gloomier: 'Yes, I have. But I haven't got the right sort of form for the customs officers to admit them through.'

He carries on arguing, but I know he has no hope. I once landed here on my way to Bangkok and then undertook an hour-long argument with a babble of bureaucrats about my five seats until we came to a compromise and agreed that I had one seat for myself and four for my wives, each dressed in white sacking and called Mrs Dipmail. Today the officials are even more bolshie.

Mitch says: 'Don't worry, they'll be on their knees kissing our asses when Iran or Iraq get itchy trigger fingers once again.'

[79]

My meeting officer resigns himself to losing the argument and joins me in the shade of the aeroplane wing to chat. He says that the Saudis are still very 'conservative'. He asked a Saudi friend why all the windows were so high up in his house and was told: 'So that a man on a camel will not be able to look inside.'

Although I like the Arabs I almost always felt depressed after my commercial visits to Arabia, particularly to Saudi. In the end, I realised why – no women. It is the presence of women in a gathering which inspires animation and jollity – it does with me, at any rate. The men-only way of life of a Muslim country makes it boring after a bit, like a vast prep school or a barracks or prison. My meeting officer tells me that the women here are beginning to work in a few offices, particularly where computers and word-processors are involved: the female mind is still associated with little more than secretarial work apparently.

Back in Bahrain, I am driven to the embassy, where I deliver the news that I have nothing to deliver, then hurry over to the hotel three furlongs away: I will just have time to have a quick swim in the hotel bathing pool. As I step on to the road outside the embassy I look the wrong way and am nearly run over by a huge lorry owned by an American construction company. It screeches to a halt. The driver, also an American, leans out of his cab: 'You **** **** !!! **** ! ****!!!' he shouts.

I am entirely in the wrong, completely my fault, no excuse. So what can one do in such circumstances but say: 'Get stuffed, c***'?

In an instant the driver is out of his cab and swinging down the handholds as nimbly as an orang-utan on being offered a banana. He looks a bit like an orang-utan as well: no neck, tubby body on short, bowed legs. He's taken his shirt off. I can admire the tattoos on his biceps: daggers dripping blood, skulls, and snakes strangling things. His chest is covered with a thick pelt of gingerish fur, amidst which two little pink nipples glow, like the eyes of an angry bear.

'What's that you're saying, mister?' he asks.

'Oops,' I reply, 'I'm so sorry, madam, I hadn't realised.'

'! – ?'

'Women's Lib, are you? I see you've burnt your bra.'
I saunter off. But it is a pretty fast saunter.

I am now back in the aeroplane, flying to Kuwait. I remember being here just after Saddam Hussein's war (Exercise Granby, we called it; the excitable Americans called it Lightning Storm and Desert Storm). The vandalised oil wells were still billowing great clouds of black smoke so that the whole of the sky seemed as if it had been heavily scribbled over with a lead pencil, and the sun glowed sombrely through the murk like a deep red tomato. The action of battle had churned up the crust of the desert so that the air was full of the finest sand: this, when mixed with the carboniferous grease and smuts from the fires, stuck on my sweating face and arms.

Day 3. On my arrival in Muscat, Mark Kettle handed me the trousers I left behind here last year. Much merriment had been caused by my fax to the embassy asking them to find them for me. We are now flying amid the towering, fluffy columns of a storm. We go through some air-pockets with some very nasty bumps. At one Katie screams and then looks frightfully angry, she is annoyed to have shown a feminine weakness. I sympathise: this aeroplane is bigger than the tiny little thing in which we fly about the Caribbean, but I still feel unease when looking down at the blanket of cloud and a hole suddenly appears in it disclosing the mountains 10,000 feet further below.

Lieut.-Colonel Reginald Dotterel-Grebe-Dotterel
(DSO, CBE)

The Royal Veterinary Society   The Cavalry Club
Amman, Jordan   London

1976 ~ Petra. It is important for a businessman in Arabia to have a representative who lives near the potential customers and is their friend. It is useful if this agent is British; the Arabs seem to trust us. It is even better if he has been a soldier; many of the older generation of Arabs have served with British soldiers, often going to Sandhurst after their initial introduction to the British way of life at Harrow and Raymond's Revue Bar. One of my agents in Arabia is Reginald. He has spent much of his life soldiering in obscure and dangerous parts of the world. He then fell in love with a Christian Lebanese, married her, but later found that a wife plus school fees for four children were not compatible with army pay. So he has become a 'contact man' here, where he has many old soldier friends.

He is small, spry, weather-beaten; his moustache and close-cut hair are of a brindled ginger, somewhat similar to mashed swedes. His braying laugh is very infectious. He always wears a tweed jacket and cavalry twill trousers, whatever the weather or latitude, but he never seems hot or uncomfortable. His main occupation is adviser on livestock breeding to sheikhs, shahs and sultans; his main hobby is worming horses. Whenever he has a spare hour or two he unpacks his drench and potions from his suitcase and soon is having a terrific argument with an incensed Viennese cabby, Cairo muleteer, Potsdam drayman, Pathan pig-sticker, Chinese ploughman or anyone else whose animal he considers needs a dose. He does not actually like the physical side of it: the gripping a horse by the nose, the insertion of the tube; it is the immense satisfaction of thinking how the walking toast-rack he has just treated would become fat and glossy and contented.

His other hobby is stealing writing paper, preferably from famous places like the Kremlin, the White House or the Vatican. His technique is to stride through the main entrance saying to any guard, in an affable but officious manner: 'Right sergeant, very good, carry on then.' It usually works, he tells me.

His other occupation is to act as contact man for a few British businessmen, of whom I am one.

Reginald and I have a day spare so we have come to Petra: 'The Rose-red city, half as old as time.' Petra was originally called Selah and was the capital of the Edomites. It is mentioned in the Second Book of Kings (chapter XIV, verse 7), when King Amaziah of Judah 'took Selah by war' and killed ten thousand of the Edomites. The Edomites deserted the city in the sixth century BC and two centuries later the Nabataeans (local desert Arabs) moved in: it became the capital of their country. Its first mention as 'Petra' was in 312 BC, when it was captured by Antigonus and looted of a great treasure. The Nabataeans became allies of Rome in 63 BC, then vassals; in AD 106 Trajan merged the country into the Roman province of Arabia. Petra had become rich through extracting toll from caravans; it increased its riches by trading in incense; its decline began in the third century through the competition of newly opened sea routes and the rival activities of the city of Palmyra. It came to European notice briefly when a Crusader fort was built on the edge of the site. When that was overrun by the Muslims it vanished from European view and became a place of legend; finally it was rediscovered in 1812 by the Swiss historian and explorer Jacob Burckhardt.

'Ideally,' Reginald said, 'one should see it first in moonlight,' but it is eight o'clock in the morning when we arrive. A little gang of pestiferous Arabs are already waiting for us. They insist that the only way up the track is on the back of their wretched nags. Reginald does not argue, as he likes any horse, so I mount one and find to my exasperation that the hirer refuses to leave go and hangs on to the leading rein.

Both names, Selah and Petra, mean 'rock', and one can see why. We pass a series of strangely shaped knolls and hillocks, some of which are surmounted by tombs, and we enter the Bab es Syk, the ravine which is the route into the city. This crack in the ground is almost a mile long and up to three hundred feet deep, and ranges in width from twenty feet to such a narrowness that the rock lips overhead almost meet and overcast the way into a warm gloom. It used to be paved, but the stream which gouged it from the rock has reclaimed its bed, although it is usually dry except for occasional flooding. The rock walls bulge and undulate and hollow in water-worn contours; there are multi-coloured streaks and strata; in places, embedded in the walls, are the remains of pottery water pipes, two thousand years old.

We turn a slight corner and suddenly see, framed to either side by the dark walls of the passage, part of an immense tomb which has been carved out of the cliff wall in front, glowing roseate in the sunlight: one hundred and thirty feet of soaring Corinthian columns, false windows, pediments and lintels carved with simple wreaths. It is the 'Treasury', so called because of the urn at the very top of the two-storey façade: it was

[83]

thought to hold treasure and is chipped by countless efforts of gunmen to puncture it so it would leak out the gold.

We are now on the Wadi Moosa, another, but wider, gorge which leads into the very heart of the old city. Our progression is eerie. The horses' hoofs are muffled by drifted sand. Tombs and houses tower to either side; hewn out of the living rock of the cliff faces, of strange designs as if built by a race of unearthly giants. The few people about look tiny in comparison. There is a great stillness, as if the whole city is holding its breath, waiting and watching. The Wadi Moosa now spreads out into a large expanse of about seven hundred acres and all around us are the remains of the city: a jumble of temples, palaces, baths, houses, a paved street following the line of the stream, once bridged at intervals; a Roman theatre, also cut out of the rock, its semicircular tiers of seats with a capacity of about three thousand. Smaller ravines lead off from the central area. They, too, are lined with houses and tombs. We leave our horses to the care of their Arab owners and scramble about the ruins. Paths and flights of steps meander over cliff faces, tiers of rock-hewn tombs and houses ascend above us; there are arches, pillars, doorways, more flights of steps, water channels and tanks. I enter some tombs, several of them smell strongly of the goats that the Arab squatters keep.

Of all this, there is not much left of the earlier Edomite town; most of the ruins now visible are either Nabataean or Roman. The Nabataean style was founded on Assyrian and Greek influences, with a dash of Egyptian and a bit of Syrian. Because of the softness of the sandstone no intricate carving was done; the effect relies on bold, simple shapes such as pillars, urns, pediments, porticoes, arches and the indigenous stepped pinnacle. Most of the later colonial building is standard Roman Empire.

The rock is not 'rose-red' anywhere, rose-pink, rather; but although that is the dominant colour at the beginning, sometimes another colour will take over, often purple or green. There are also remarkable multicolour effects: tiny layers of colour make the rock wall seem woven in finest taffeta or watered silk, or in sheets, as if the tombs have been wallpapered with rainbow. The whole place is utterly alien, the style and size of the constructions and excavations, the iridescent colours of the rock, the feeling that we are being watched, resentfully, by the spirits of those who lived here so long ago.

In 1976, when I went with Reginald, there were very few other people: some Arab squatters inhabiting the tombs, about a score of tourists. The place has since become packed with tourists and hotels have been built nearby.

Olaf Ø. Shag

Steinkjer
Nord-Trøndelag
Norway

1954 ~ The Jotunheimen Mountains, Norway. Nowadays, when skiing or mountaineering, people dress up in all-in-one rubber suits, as tight and as colourful as the skins of tropical frogs. In my youth one generally disguised oneself as a gamekeeper: Norfolk jacket, knickerbockers, long hairy stockings, heavy leather boots. And perhaps all this would be surmounted by a deerstalker cap: Olaf, our guide, being a Norseman, wore a knitted hat with a bobble on top instead. He was an ornithologist and mountain climber: nice enough, but never washed – even we noticed. Once he had taken his boots and socks off and exposed his feet, swollen and knobbled and green, like pickled gherkins, one could understand why he rarely had a bath; few people would want to sit in the same bath as those feet.

Jacques Robin

Forgeron

Montrozier
Gorges du Tarn

1947 ~ Massif Central, France. Monsieur Robin was my childhood hero. He had vast shoulders upon which had been placed a microscopic head, of the same shape, size, colour and bristly texture as a coconut. Whenever I arrived to stay with my French cousins in their castle in the Massif Central I would unpack and then make a bee-line for Monsieur Robin's forge. The colossal muscles of his arms would be lit up by the glow of the red-hot shoes in the dark, cobwebby and sooty recesses of his forge. They were ox shoes. Each ox needed eight shoes, one for each hooflet. Oxen hate being shod: they have to be restrained in a wooden frame; once they have been goaded into it, straps are passed under their bodies and they would be heaved off their feet by Monsieur Robin turning the roller windlasses. Even then the oxen would struggle and kick, and Monsieur Robin's cursing filled me with admiration.

Cattle have long memories, and a great capacity for resentment. That is why a cattle farmer will get another farmer to nose-ring his bulls. The oxen would pull tumbrels and waggons through the cobbled streets of the village, or haul ploughs in the adjacent fields, and whenever they passed Monsieur Robin their heads would lower and sway towards him, and their eyes would narrow.

I last saw him in 1984. He was old, wizened and bent. Finally his muscles seemed in proportion to his head. But he was still in his forge, fiddling about with a solder, mending a lawn-mower. 'No more oxen,' he said, 'everyone has those . . . ing tractors nowadays.'

He pointed to a stack of ox yokes in a corner: 'No longer needed, only useful as kindling wood.'

They were a beautiful shape, polished with years of use, so I took a couple home.

An antique-dealing friend saw them: 'I'll give you 50 quid each for any more of those you can get.'

I telephoned Monsieur Robin and offered him a tenner for each of his yokes. He proved that his cursing, unlike his body, had not deteriorated. There was a torrent of expletives as he told me that he had just chopped up the last one.

[86]

> Martin Paterson Donnelly
>
> COURTAULDS LTD
>
> Foleshill Road
>
> Coventry

1950 ~ Home.   The New Zealanders are reputed to be very pleasant but rather mousy and dull – all Women's Institute and bowling clubs and knitting competitions. Yet Rommel said that the New Zealand troops were the most fearsome of all his opponents: remorseless in attack, brave and stoic in defence; every man with an unbreakable morale and self-sufficient in all such skills as shooting, driving or orienteering. As a schoolboy, I reckoned Martin Donnelly to be an epitome of all this: gentle, mild and kind, and a brilliant cricketer. He had played for New Zealand, Oxford University and Courtaulds Ltd (when he was working for the company). He was a left-hand bat and a slow left-arm orthodox bowler: nominated The Wisden Cricketer of the Year, 1948. He autographed my cricket bat. As a result my batting average almost doubled – from three runs to five.

1998 September ~ CENTRAL EUROPE

Day 1.   As Queen's Messengers, Craik and I have visited most of the former communist capitals of Central and Eastern Europe – Bucharest, Budapest, Bratislava, Belgrade, Moscow, Zagreb, Warsaw, Sofia, Kiev, Prague – and all we saw of most of them was the tarmac of their airports: having handed over the diplomatic bags to the meeting officers we returned to base in the same aeroplanes. And so we have decided to take our wives and explore a bit of what we have only seen from the air: the vineyards of Franconia, the forest of Bohemia, the plains of Transdanubia, the hills of Moravia,

[87]

even the cabbage fields of Slovakia. Two and a half thousand miles in all, our main ports of call being Prague, Budapest and Vienna, but with interesting stops on the way.

The car is ready, my Land-Rover Discovery, with all the things obligatory for travel there: a First Aid kit, a fire extinguisher, a red warning triangle; I have a spare set of bulbs and belts, some cans of oil and the AA guide. My route is planned, the stopping places are booked – the priority being that any place we stay has safe parking for our car.

We are on the Dover–Calais ferry by seven o'clock. Last time I was on this was as a guest of my Foreign Office driver, as he and I took a van of diplomatic mail to Paris. Now I am part of the less-privileged mob. Instead of the discreet luxury of the Drivers' Saloon we are in a crowded area of benches and small tables, having breakfast. This is a cup of coffee and a McDonald's bun. It is the first time I have ever eaten one and I am quite amazed, it seems to be made entirely of layers of plastic of different colours and textures: foamed polystyrene on the outside (bread), then a layer of something shiny and pink (ham), imitation cork flooring ('hamburger'), thin sheets of green cellophane (lettuce) and three hard green disks – gaming counters? No, sliced cucumber. Fortunately it tastes of nothing. Even the yellow smear in the middle (mustard) tastes of nothing.

Day 2.   We are staying in a pension in Prague. It is only £16 a night per head, and is reasonably clean and central and near a tram stop. It is also pretty spartan. The building was once the house of a rich family: the façade is elegant, the heavy entrance door opens to a flight of steps with the remains of a mural on the vaulted ceiling. There is an ambience of faded gentility. Our rooms are connected with a small lobby. It all smells of cheap carpet. The beds are small. The lavatories and showers in each room were also built for midgets. But the young landlord, Vladimir, and his pretty wife Dana, are helpful and anxious.

I park the car in the courtyard, we unpack and sally out to look around. It is getting late so we have time for only a short walk to reconnaissance our environments, firstly the four hundred yards to the Number 22 tram stop in Náměstí Square. Vlad the Landlord tells us that this tram will be able to take us to most of the places we want to see over the next three days. Another short walk, and we are standing in front of the National Museum and beside a statue of King Wenceslas, mounted on a horse and brandishing a sword. We are looking down the whole length of Wenceslas Square. This is about half a mile long and sixty-five yards wide, avenued with trees and assorted houses, cinemas, restaurants and shops, all slightly scruffy: not really a square, more like a down-market Champs Elysées. It has been the centre of recent Czech history: where the new state of Czecho-Slovakia was declared in 1918, where the state was abolished by German tanks in 1939, where Russian tanks corralled in 1968, where the student-martyr Jan Palach incinerated himself in protest against communist rule and where, twenty years later (1989), half a million Czechs massed in protest against police brutality, the rally which led to the overthrow of communism.

We had dinner in a cosy restaurant within a brick-vaulted basement. The poor waiter was charming and solicitous: he had the time; we were the only customers. The menu was huge, but most of the food came from tins, even the 'famous' (to the waiter) Prague ham was revealed as a pepped-up spam. The 'Goulash with Dumplings' turned out to be slices of stodgy bread and fibrous lumps, the former floating upon a heavy gravy, the latter lurking within its depths like the blind porpoises in the murky waters of the lower Amazon.

Day 3. We spent all day exploring Prague. The city was once the capital of the Kingdom of Bohemia and now is the capital of the Czech Republic. It started off as a place of defence and a centre of trade, and owes its importance and beauty to its promotion as the capital of the Holy Roman Empire under Charles IV, in the fourteenth century. To the British its main historical impact was religious: firstly the schism between the Hussites, the 'protesting' followers of Jan Hus, and the Catholic Church; secondly the 'Defenestration of Prague' in 1618, when the Protestant citizens of Prague threw the bureaucrats of the Catholic rulers, the Hapsburgs, out of the windows of Hrdcany Castle, thus contributing to the Thirty Years War. The first battle in that war, the romantically named Battle of the White Mountain (1620) resulted in the Bohemians becoming vassals of Hapsburg Austria. Hitler spared

Prague from his bombs, intending 'Golden Prague', 'The City of a thousand spires', to be the capital of his Centralised European Community. After Hitler, the Soviet communists; then the 'Prague Spring', a period of liberalisation under Alexander Dubček, crushed by the invasion of the Soviet army in 1968; finally freedom, followed by the amiable (but unwise) separation of the Czech and Slovak Republics.

Prague is a city of roofscapes: with spires, steeples, turrets, domes, 'wedge' roofs (like upside-down axe-heads) and gables. Dominating it all is the Citadel on an escarpment above the River Vltava; dominant in the Citadel are the spires and belfry of its cathedral and the 'thousand-eyed' windowed walls of its Castle/palace. The Citadel also includes a complex of living quarters for royalty, livery, laity, clergy and the military; churches and chapels, defence towers, libraries and stables, gateways, fountains, statues, courtyards and alleyways. The Citadel is the topmost part of the Castle District, one of the four distinct areas which form the ancient heart of the city, the other districts being the Lesser Town, below the Castle, the Old Town across the river and the New Town ('New' is fourteenth century).

After breakfast we took Tram 22 to go to the Citadel. The trams are pay-as-you-enter, with slippery seats of moulded plastic and smiling and nodding passengers. We first rambled in the Royal Garden running alongside the north of the whole area. The buildings within, a 'Ball-game' house and the Royal Summer Palace, are painted with *sgraffito* (two-tone painting on plastered walls). Amid the box-hedged convolutions of the formal gardens before the Summer Palace is a fountain known as the 'Singing Fountain' (1620). If you are near it you can hear a faint beating chime as the bronze bowl reverberates to the running water. I found a Turkish hazel – at last. I have planted several small saplings at home to encourage dormice but have never seen a full-grown tree. The example I found is quite attractive, with a deeply fissured, corky bark, about sixty feet high; but the nuts had been shed – it must have had a harvest which could be measured in tons rather than bushels. Craik said that when mine finally starts cropping I'll be overrun with grey squirrels and crows.

The adjacent buildings are dominated by St Vitus's Cathedral, whose twin Gothic spires and tiered Baroque tower can be seen for miles. It took six hundred years to be built, from its inception by King John of Luxembourg to its consecration in 1929. During this long period of construction it was the site of about thirty coronations of the rulers of Bohemia; fifteen of the rulers are buried here. Within, it is a lofty Gothic soaring, four hundred feet long and a hundred and ten feet high.

There are many interesting side chapels. In one, off the nave, there is the remarkably vulgar tomb of St John of Nepomuk, crafted from two tons of silver. 'That's solid silver,' I said to Craik. 'Can't be. Look at that angel, she must be hollow, she's got a distinct dent on her shoulder, like a battered plastic doll,' he replied.

My puritan genes cannot help resisting all this show-offiness and imagery and subconsciously look for reasons to disapprove ('if you melt down all this bullion you'd get enough to feed a million starving people for a year . . . which would give them the chance of breeding yet another million to starve'). As I pondered, an American woman near me sneezed. 'Pardon me,' she said apologetically, looking up at the silver saint.

There are panels which depict allegorical tableaux of Good versus Evil; the Goodies are all pretty damsels, the Baddies are all crabby old ladies badly in need of brassières. That is rather unfair. In real life it is the young maidens who often need reproof; it is the old grannies who are knitting for the Third World and running meals-on-wheels and orphaned kittens' homes. Further down the aisle is the chapel of St Wenceslas. Above, its walls are covered with Gothic and Renaissance paintings; below, they are plated with a crazy-paving of slices of semiprecious stones. The sepulchre of the saint is comparatively simple, about the size and shape of a chicken coop, covered with a scarlet and golden pall. The whole thing is interesting but over-sugary. Much more interesting to a schoolboy's mind is a bronze door handle which is thought to be the one St Wenceslas clung to as he tried (unsuccessfully) to gain sanctuary from his fratriciding brother, Boleslav.

The Good King Wenceslas (907–929) is a bit confusing: there were several King Wenceslases, but none of them was the Saint, who was not a King, but a Royal Duke. He was not even particularly good, except when compared with his family, the Premyslids, the first dynastic rulers of Prague: his mother Dragomira, for example, murdered her mother-in-law in a fit of jealousy; his brother, Boleslav the Cruel, murdered him. Wenceslas's martyrdom was attributed to his mild (i.e. ineffective) resistance to a pagan revival in his principality, but basically it was the culmination of one of the many family feuds. He was stabbed by Boleslav as he entered a church to attend mass.

We climb two hundred and eighty-seven steps up a spiral stairway in a lookout tower. Copper cocks crow from the gable ends below us, and gargoyles grin or snarl; further below them the spires and steeples of the city bristle like the spears of some defensive army; amidst them, the river meanders in and out of view and glides under its bridges.

We clamber down the tower steps. An impatient German jostles peevishly at us as we pass, he has already climbed a hundred and twenty steps and is purple with the effort.

'Don't fuss, only another hundred and sixty-seven steps more,' I advise him, kindly.

We leave the Citadel and zigzag down some terraced gardens to the lower part of the Castle District, to St Nicholas's church. This was built by the Jesuits when they were trying to counteract the dourness and dullness of Protestantism with exciting opulence. Outside, it has a pedimented and curving façade culminating in a dome and single belfry tower, both covered with verdigris-green copper. Inside, it is what interior designers call 'busy': the most ornate example of High Baroque I have ever seen, a plethora of swags and curlicues, hardly a straight line or flat surface anywhere. The basis is a nave built on a ground plan of three transverse ovals; above is the dome, two hundred feet high. The ceiling fresco in the main nave glorifies the life of the patron saint. It was painted by K.L. Kracker (never heard of him) and is one of the largest paintings in Europe, being 15,00 square metres. Its decoration and *trompe-l'oeil* merges with the upper architecture so that it is hard to discern where the painting ends and the church begins and so somehow one is drawn into the aerial scene and becomes part of it. Below, all is a busyness of sculptural activity: gilded angels flanking pictures, devils being slain, saints doing the slaying, or reading, or blessing, everywhere cherubs buzz around being useful, pointing out directions or the doings of good deeds by other statues, or holding up books, or offering croziers, or just acting as train bearers with the hems of episcopal robes. The cherubs are uncommonly stout; their tiny wings seem even more futile than those of bumble bees for carrying their chubby burdens. We walk up the main nave flanked by colossal statues of – somewhat puzzlingly – King Cyrus of Persia, the Emperors Constantine and Theodosius II and a fellow with a scourge and ball and chain. Even larger are the four statues in the corners below the dome: the Teachers of the Eastern Church lean over us, each higher than a London bus from toe to mitre. The Rococo pulpit is stuck on the side of a pillar like a swallow's nest. Its basic material is a 'marble' which I say is coloured mauve, Dominie says is dirty pink, Margaret says is raspberry and Craik says that whatever it is, it is pretty ghastly. This material bulges out like a bolster between the golden tendrils which clamber over it; also golden are the cherubs which swarm among them like bees upon a pavlova.

One of the many side chapels is dedicated to St Barbara, the patron saint of 'Contented Death', also of fireworks makers, artillery men and grave-diggers; she was a defender against lightning strikes and impenitence. Sadly, the church of Rome has decided that she never existed. But I'll believe in her, to keep her going – like fairies.

Near the church is the palace of General Count Albrecht Wallenstein, who was the commander of the Imperial Catholic Armies during most of the Thirty Years War. His successes led him to get *folie de la grandeur*: he built an impertinently intrusive palace next to the Imperial one, he began to plot against the Emperor. It was the Emperor who had the last laugh, he had Wallenstein killed – the assassins were an Englishman, a Scotsman and an Irishman. We walked around his garden, amid the peacocks and statuary and wall paintings: it was almost all second-rate – the *nouveau-riche* soldier had been conned by the art dealers.

The city is teeming with people, many of them Japanese tourists. Perhaps their archipelago is getting so full of people they have to send a percentage away, to leave room for the remainder. The Czechs are very friendly and not at all what I thought. I had imagined them either to be squat and slavonic, or Bohemianally mysterious, with long flowing capes, ditto beards, smoking cigarettes on long holders and with very pretty and rather dirty mistresses. They are rarely those, but are almost everything else: tall and blond, ginger, swarthy, thin and melancholy, fat and jolly; basically northern, most of them would look more at home in Colchester than in Paris or Rome.

We went to a concert in the evening, in the National Museum at the near end of Wenceslas Square. The programme said that it was being held in the 'Inner Staircase of the Central Hall'. When we entered we were each handed a cushion. We followed other members of the audience and found that we were expected to sit on a flight of wide marble steps. In the central landing the musicians performed, firstly four fellows who played a string quartet by Mozart; then they were joined by a tubby little Japanese female for Dvořák's Piano Quintet in A major. Surprisingly I enjoyed it all, even the Dvořák.

Before it began I had a chat with the two stout American women in trews who sat on the step below me. As the one in front lowered herself onto her purple cushion she resembled a tartan balloon landing on a grouse moor.

Day 5. We have just had dinner in one of Prague's taverns. Everyone but me felt tired and decided to take Tram 22 back to our digs, but I have decided to walk; it will only take about an hour (standing about in a tram queue could take about that long and feel even longer).

The medieval Charles Bridge over the River Vltava is 1700 feet long and thirty feet wide, it has sixteen arches and along the parapets there are thirty statues or tableaux totalling seventy-five figures in all. There are medieval towers guarding each end of the bridge, with both witch's hat turrets and wedge roofs, the Old Town Bridge Tower at one end is considered the finest medieval tower in Europe. During the day it is crammed with people: pedestrians, peddlers, buskers; this morning there was a superb jazz band. Now, in the evening, it is quiet and eerie. To either side of me the avenue of statues stands silhouetted against the moonlit sky, sombre and brooding, or in martyred agony, or with arms upraised in appeal or admonition or warning or blessing. The clouds passing over the moon make the graven faces change expression: eyes gloom and blink in hollowed sockets. After I have walked past the figures seem to close in behind me, and lean together, and talk about me, and look away when I glance over my shoulder.

Now through cobbled streets to Old Town Square. I stop to look at the Town Hall clock. The skeletal figure of Death beside it suddenly pulls on the rope he is holding. It gives me a regular turn. He raises and inverts the hourglass which he is holding in his other hand. Two windows open above the clock and the Twelve Apostles appear and dodder slowly round in procession. A cock appears cuckoo-clock-wise and crows, then the clock strikes ten.

I quit, with Death grinning toothily at me through the gloom: along the half-mile length of Wenceslas Square, past the National Museum, along the silent streets where my shoes clatter on the cobbles, through the now-familiar lawns and hedges of Náměstí Square, up America Road; shout up to our window, Dominie looks out and throws me the keys. They have been back only half an hour.

Day 6. On the way from Prague to Český Krumlov we stopped at České Budějovice ('Budweis', to its medieval German settlers) and had a drink in the centre, Náměstí Přemysla Otakara II, one of Europe's largest town squares: basically Baroque, with a large fountain in the centre and elegant buildings mostly erected during three hundred years of German burgher rule. Obviously I tried out the local brew, 'Budweiser', whose name has been usurped by an American company for their stewed and filtered gnat's pee. This original Budweiser actually tastes of beer, and has colour, and is alcoholic.

Český Krumlov is wonderful, magic, real fairytale stuff. The towers and walls of a massive castle are reflected in the placid waters of a river. Bells chime from churches and towers. There are cobbled squares where drinking fountains trickle. Little timbered houses line crooked alleyways. Looming above the hodge-podge of their tiled roofs one can see the high pastures and hanging woodlands of the Sumava Hills.

The town began to flourish in early medieval times, when a fortification was built beside a loop of the River Vltava to protect an important ferry crossing used by merchants. The fortress became a castle and the village below it expanded into a town during the fourteenth century. During the Hussite wars in the next century the town became an important point of defence for the Catholics. Time passed, generally the town prospered; to its Gothic was added Renaissance, then Baroque, Rococo and Classicism – later, the penury of the communist years inhibited mass rebuilding, so that now the town has earned a rare status as a Unesco World Cultural Monument.

The majority of the town is in the pear-shaped area of land within the loop of river, the castle is built on a clifftop on the other side of the waters. We cross the wooden bridge, walk up a cobbled street, lined with shops, step through the main portals of the castle, cross a bridge over a 'bear moat', where a quartet of bored bears sit amid their turds and eat stale buns; then through an uphill passage, wide enough to take horses, into a large courtyard dominated by the round tower and with walls of *sgraffito*. By the entrance arch we can see the wear once made by sentries' boots. Like the Dukes of Atholl, who are privileged to keep their own tiny army, so the Schwarzenbergs of Krumlov Castle were allowed their own troop of men: dressed in Napoleonic uniform, the twelve men used to tramp about at intervals, one of them would sound a bugle at nine o'clock every morning from the round tower. There are guided tours for the interior of the castle, but all in German or Czech, and entailing long waits in queues, so we carry on alone. There are two smaller courtyards within the body of the castle, rather like wells within the tall, surrounding walls and made extra sinister by the heraldry, this time a ubiquitous crest which depicts a screaming head with its eyes being pecked out by a raven.

The main defensive and residential body of the castle is separated from its leisure buildings and gardens by a steep gorge; this is crossed by a beautiful three-tiered bridge, banistered with statues. Just on the other side is the theatre, which we have just entered. It is an extraordinarily ornate Rococo arrangement, one of the few of such stages which still has its original equipment: scenery, scene-shifting machinery and wardrobe. As the guide book said: 'An ingenious system of flies and flats meant that a typical comic opera of the kind the theatre specialised in could have more than forty scene changes without interrupting the action.'

To bed. From our bedroom windows in the Hotel Dvořák we can see the castle walls reflected in the river just below us; high above us, on the clifftop on the other bank, the great tower looms against the night sky. We can hear ducks quacking. A bell chimes. There is a splash as some fish jumps.

Day 7. The two-hour drive from Český Krumlov to Telč was mostly through undulating, wooded countryside through which our road meandered, almost traffic-free, avenued with apple trees. In Telč we are in the Hotel Ná Hrázi, stark and modern with a reception desk like the information office of an airport and bedrooms furnished simply in black and white, but it is cheap and clean and a convenient one-minute walk to the entrance gate of the town.

A guide book says that the last exciting event in Telč was a great fire in 1530. This wiped out the whole town, including the castle. It was all immediately rebuilt, in Renaissance style, and nothing has happened here since. As a result it is a perfect museum piece, set in a time warp; like Český Krumlov it has been designated a World Cultural Monument by Unesco.

We walk through one of the two medieval gate towers, up a cobbled street, and find ourselves in a long, trapezoidal square. All sides of the square are bounded by arcades, upon which the houses rest; each house has a different gable, in style rather Dutch to me – everything is painted in pastel colours. The castle takes up one end of the square, an ornate fountain dominates the other. Beside the castle there is a large church, which, being of stone, like the entrance towers, escaped the conflagration. Telč is beautiful, but it seems dead, with no more liveliness than the painted scenery on a stage. The square is almost empty of people, the few that are there, even the children, seem bored and listless. It echoes from side to side. There aren't even any pigeons or sparrows pecking about the cobbles. We want to go inside the castle. It has a magnificent Golden Hall ceiling whose gilded panels frame blue octagons; from the postcards, they look rather like plaques of Wedgwood. As we approach the castle a bearded churl swings the gates shut in our faces, in spite of our pointing out the sign that says 'OPEN UNTIL 5'; it is four o'clock at present. The church is also shut.

After buying a few postcards we ramble around the lawns and lakes of the castle garden and do a reconnaissance for dinner (we choose a pleasant tavern near the hotel, just within the gates), then wander back to the hotel to bath and read or write before dinner.

[97]

Goose legs for dinner, not bad; the legs of the mini-skirted waitress were pretty good as well, Craik and I agree.

Day 8. At present we are driving through Slovakia. We have realised that we have seen hardly any animals in our journeying through ex-communist Europe, not even a squashed hedgehog: one hare, a small covey of partridge, a few deer; no livestock in the fields, presumably they are all enclosed in some of the hangar-like buildings we occasionally see next to a farm. Also slightly eerie are the fields of about-to-be-harvested sunflowers, silent hosts of dead plants, still standing, man high, their blackened, drooping heads all facing the same way, as of armies which have been struck by a sudden burst of nuclear fire.

We have reached the outskirts of Budapest. We will spend two days here, then go on to Vienna for a couple more, then back home via Rothenburg ob der Tauber.

Day 13. The Hotel Eisenhut in Rothenburg ob der Tauber is one of the famous small hotels of Europe. I park the car on the cobbles below the sign of an iron helmet (the 'Eisenhut'). Inside, it is all Bavarian *Gemutlichkeit*: cosy and stolid, it has heavy wooden furniture and a carved oaken staircase, overhead beams, panelling, stone pillars and arches; decorating the walls are oil paintings, swords, armour, pewter plates and brass candlesticks; rugs and carpets are scattered about.

I hurry up to the reception desk, behind which scowls a man in a suit and a pinch-faced blonde. 'Good afternoon,' I say breezily, 'we have two rooms booked here. I was last here over sixty years ago, in August 1937. Before I was born! My parents were staying here. One evening they saw a stork flying overhead. Nine months later I arrived!'

They couldn't care a monkey's fuck.

'Have you evidence of your booking?' asks the churl. He looks disappointed when I whisk out the fax confirming it. He and the blonde get into a huddle and confer.

Finally, Churl reluctantly agrees: 'Yes, there is a double room for Mr and Mrs Courtauld, and another room – an eyebrow twitches – for Mr Colonel and Mrs Craik.'

'Actually, it should say Colonel and Mrs Craik,' Craik points out, rather testily.

Once more Churl and Peevish are filled with the wildest indifference.

A porter takes the car to park it in the hotel's garage; another porter takes us to our rooms. As we walk down the corridors, creaky with old boarding, I keep an eye out for a sign on any of the doors. But no, there is no blue plaque saying:

GEORGE
COURTAULD
CONCEIVED
WITHIN

Rothenburg ob der Tauber is one of the most complete of Europe's walled medieval cities. The appearance is slightly bogus as the eastern part of the city was flattened by an allied bombardment near the end of the war. Fortunately the historic and beautiful centre was undamaged, and the destroyed part of the city was rebuilt to the ancient plans. Rothenburg's wealth was confirmed in 1274 when King Rudolf of Hapsburg granted it a charter to become a 'Free Imperial City' of the German Empire, under the Emperor's special protection. The resulting prosperity, brought about by its position as a trading centre, enabled it, by 1400, to rule a 'mini-state' of 250 square miles. The burghers then meddled in politics, disaster was only averted during the Thirty Years War by the famous 'Meistertrunk' (Master draught) when the invading enemy wagered the destruction of the city against the ability of ex-mayor Georg Nusch to drink 3.25 litres of wine in one gulp. The drink was drunk and the city saved. In 1802 Rothenburg lost its independence and was incorporated into the Kingdom of Bavaria.

The city is still almost completely girdled round by its wall, two and a half kilometres of it. Near the upper level there is a covered walkway. As we proceed along it in Indian file we can look, on one side, through firing slits to the moat and the gorges of the Tauber, to the other side we can look down into gardens and back yards, or over the huddled mass of fish-scaled tiles.

We reach one of the city gates. It is remarkably complex: a moated bastion of two outer courtyards and seven gates, the road through them being dog-legged to interrupt artillery fire. We descend down a tower into a street and walk to the main church, St Jakob's, its Gothic/Lutheran simplicity startling compared with the Baroque opulence of the previous fortnight. Built in the early 1300s it was an important source of pilgrimage, holding a relic of the Holy Blood. There are two medieval altarpieces, painted and gilded over the main altar; even more remarkable is the altarpiece of the Twelve Apostles by Friedrich Herlin (1466) – plain, woodwormed and impressive. To get to it one climbs a flight of steps at the west end, behind the organ loft. The altarpiece, of plain, uncoloured wood, is a large and superb triptych based on the Last Supper. It is shaming that I am reminded of another local art form, the cuckoo clock. The thirteenth-century reliquary hangs above it, a crucifix holding the vial of the Holy Blood, just visible behind a windowing of rock crystal.

Day 14. Home, in the late afternoon, having driven a total of 2400 miles. The White Cliffs of Dover looked superb. But having landed back in our island we thought everything seemed so small, and so crowded, and so cut up by hedges, and the driving so slow and meandering and indecisive.

Kevin Crane, MP

The House of Commons
Whitehall
London

1991 Caracas. 'Aren't you the Minister of Health?' I asked as he lit up his third cigarette within half an hour.

'Shut up,' he said. 'I get snide remarks like that from every Matron I meet.'

It was two o'clock in the morning. We were in the VIP lounge of Caracas airport. I have rarely met a man with such early-morning energy: pacing about, fidgeting, bouncing off the walls like a squash ball.

'Who's that beautiful blonde sitting on your diplomatic bags, not part of your regulation issue, I presume?'

'Yes she is,' I replied, 'she's my escort.'

'What's that mean?'

'If there is any sign of danger, I fling myself on top of the diplomatic bags, and she flings herself on top of me.'

He mused for a bit, then: 'As your employer I order you to change places with me – you can be Minister of Health for a bit – and after a while I want you to suddenly shout "BANG!".'

I said that my only boss was the Queen or her representative, the Foreign Minister, so, sorry, no, she's mine.

This Crane was not in the remotest like another MP who by coincidence not only had the same name but also was with me and the same escort a year ago in the same time and place. This earlier Crane was quiet and tired and seemingly jetlagged, but he was more on the ball than I thought, for when I read his published diaries later he too had admired my escort – he described her as 'a true phew-wotta-scorcher'. He described me as 'a large man in a rumpled suit'. It could have been worse. For a lot of people in his diary, it was.

JOHN C. REEVE, 26
Ryder Street
St James's
Piccadilly

Pratts

1998 ~ London. To break up the boring two-day sequence (Warsaw and back today; Moscow and back tomorrow) my friend John is kindly putting me up for the night in his flat near St James's Street. He has bought an oil painting of an orang-utan squatting on a log.

'An ancestral portrait, I presume,' I say.

THE LAST TRAVELS OF A FAT BULLDOG

'Of course,' he replies, 'I come from a very old family.'
You cannot outwit a good lawyer.

Herbert R. Brambling

c/o The Heritage Domestic Agency
255, Knightsbridge Mews
London SW1

1978 ~ Saudi Arabia.   Herbert R. Brambling was young for a butler, but
as neatly dressed as one would expect. I met him on a flight to Saudi
Arabia, where he was to take over the domestic staff of one of the
younger of the Saudi princes.

'His Highness has recently married and I have a contract to work for
him four years, by which time I will have fully trained all the domestic
staff in his six palaces and hunting lodge, and given advice on where
and how to live in London, New York and Paris.'

'I should think you will probably have to train *him* as well.'

'You are completely correct, sir. Our agency specialises in tactfully
telling the rich but perhaps not yet fully *au fait* "men of the world" what to
do and what not to do. I will be instructing him on what to wear on formal
and informal occasions, where to buy his clothes and accessories, even, if
necessary, where to purchase a racehorse and how to behave in the
paddock, or where to learn to shoot or fish or hunt, and all the etiquette
that goes with all these different activities.'

'Have you been doing this sort of thing for long?'

'My family have always been in domestic service, sir. My father
started as a footman for the Duke of Leeds, my grandfather was head
steward in charge of the royal railway carriages of the personal railway
train of Her Majesty Queen Victoria. It is a tradition in my family that
an ancestor was cup-bearer to His Majesty King Richard I, a very hot-
tempered gentleman, I believe [do I trace a glimmer of self-mocking in
those mild grey eyes?]. But there is little demand for senior domestic

[102]

staff at present, except for pop stars and footballers, and they are not agreeable to my inclinations, so I joined the agency twelve years ago and to be honest, sir, I could now afford a butler for myself, if that was to my choosing. But it is not.'

He and I had an amiable but long argument on the merits of wearing national clothes rather than Western ones; then the aeroplane landed and we parted. While I was met by Land-Rover and escort, he was collected by a lilac Rolls Royce.

'I bet that car will be a different colour by next month,' I said to him as I walked past.

'By tomorrow,' he replied.

1998 October ~ SCANDINAVIA

Day 1. A busy two days: six aeroplane flights, four bag exchanges, at Copenhagen, Oslo, Vilnius and Stockholm. Of them all, I only have any spare time in Stockholm. I am sorry about Copenhagen, as I have lots of friends and relations there, some quite unusual, like Cousin Axel who once lived in a fireplace in the Royal Palace, and Varvara, the 'Great Dane', who has just sent me her biography of her mother, complete with appendices listing some of her horses and lovers: thirty-seven of the former; forty-three of the latter. Varvara is known as the 'Great Dane' as she is six foot two inches high and wears heels five inches high.

Of Vilnius – the only thing I know about Lithuania is a conversation Ronnie Capel Cure told me he had overhead in his club:

First Venerable Old Boy: I've got to go to Lithuania, have you heard of it?
Second Venerable Old Boy: Three of my friends used to own it.
First VOB: What's it like?
Second VOB: Good shooting.
First VOB: What are the Lithuanians like?
Second VOB: Good beaters.

Day 2. At present I am having breakfast in my hotel in Stockholm. It is a healthy help-yourself buffet: platters laden with slices of anaemic meats and fat-free cheeses, heaps of fruit with the taste of distilled water, bowls full of gritty and grainy cereals designed to scour rapidly through the human intestines like shovel-loads of gravel. I am sitting facing the pavement, looking through two windows at the pedestrians hurrying past to their offices. It must be cold: people are wearing gloves and coats; many are balloon-bodied and spindle-shanked in puffa jackets. Here comes a woman in boots and rucksack, head well down as she strides on; another woman, invisible amidst an enveloping green shawl except for long, lòng legs in white stockings; a threadbare man, drifting; two animated women, chattering. There is a man scowling at me – balding, heavily built, coarse and rather degenerate features, wearing a brass-buttoned boating jacket with a spotted red handker-chief tucked in the breast pocket . . . It's my jacket! . . . It's me! It's my reflection in the looking-glass between the windows.

Until I was about fifteen I could never be taught anything apart from History and English. I sat behind my desk, staring at my teachers, absolutely amazed that anyone could be so boring: 'Mensa-mensa-mensam, mensorum-mensis-mensis, table-table-table, to-a-table of-a-table by-with-or-from-a-table'; 'the second personal pronoun of the past participle of the pluperfect persuant of *pissoir* is *pissey-vous*'; 'The exportation of waistcoat buttons from Belgium was 36,789 gross in 1877 – by 1921 this trade had increased to 432,447. However, their importation of mouse fur increased by 257 per cent in 1922. So what was the number I first thought of, Courtauld? Well, boy?! Wake up! Wake up! You're always half asleep!' By the end of each lesson my mind was completely devoid of any of the expensively paid-for information. I filled the ensuing blank in my head with things I found much more interesting: the meanings of the Egyptian hieroglyphs; the names of every British butterfly and bird; the family trees of the Classic and Teutonic gods and goddesses; the different types of sword, spear and pike; the Chinese dynasties; all the verses of *The Charge of the Light Brigade* and *Lars Porsena* of Clusium; the rigging of a sailing ship.

I learnt the last from a book which is still one of my favourites: *Sailing*

Ships and Rigging by Harold Underhill. This gives the spars, sails and cordage of pretty well any British sailing boat and ship, from the rich man's yacht, such as the ketch and yawl, to the working man's vessel, such as the Thames barge, the brig and the snow, to the exotic – the four-mast jackass barque, the three-mast fore-and-aft schooner, the hermaphrodite brig and the barquentine. Because of an illegitimate liaison, my family secretly owned the *Cutty Sark* for a brief period so I decided to learn the full rigging of that most beautiful of ships, the three-masted 'tea clipper': all the sails from, fore and aft, the flying jib to the spanker, and from aloft to below, the main skysail to the top-mast staysail; there was not a bit of cordage I did not know from the top-gallant bunt-lines to the fore-topmast-staysail halyards. However, practically, most of my seamanship was as one of a crew of sixteen, rowing a lumbering great clinker-built whaler up and down the Moray Firth, with oars as big as telegraph poles and an incontinent mongrel as the ship's mascot.

Stockholm is a city built on thirteen islands, and as such it is a city of bridges and boats. From almost every angle one can see masts and funnels: a good place to satisfy my liking for ships.

I sally out with the contents of my 'Sweden' flowerpot. I have about sixty flowerpots on a shelf by my study. Each one contains items I may need for different places I visit: city maps, guide books, £5 worth of local currency, calling cards of friends and so on. My flowerpot for Sweden includes an old phrase book, which I deduce belonged to my grandfather as phrases include 'I want a room with an open fire/and a piano', 'Please stretch these gloves', 'I want a pince-nez with a gold frame/and a cord'.

'*Känner ni till någon bra twätterska?*' means 'Do you know of any good washerwoman?' I'd like to meet a *twätterska*, she sounds more fun than your normal washerwoman.

Outside, it is sharp with a cold wind; there are no clouds, the sun is so bright off the waters that I cannot see properly and my eyes sting and weep in the glare. But Stockholm is a delightful place to walk in – I feel light-hearted in the cold and the clarity, not leaden and stuffy, as I often do in Rome or Athens or Madrid. Perhaps it is some inherited empathy. It is eight o'clock, everything is shut until ten, so I'll wander off and look at the three-masted sailing ship I have previously seen only from afar.

The autumn colours are vivid. I walk past three lines of birch. In the wind they are all of a-shimmer like a troupe of chorus girls in dresses of golden sequins. They exude a slight scent of autumn, it mingles with the smell of the sea. As feminine, but in a different way, is the sentry outside the main portals of the Royal Palace: dressed baggily in a slightly too large uniform and sloppy spats, and hugging a rifle as if it were a teddy bear rather than an instrument of Death, she stares worriedly at me as I stare at her. I do not approve of women being armed, but she looks so inefficient that she is rather sweet.

Gulls mew overhead; a small flotilla of mallard manoeuvre by a bridge. I cross another one. There are men fishing from it – for salmon, one of them tells me. Salmon fishing in the centre of a capital city! The fisherman has a line as long as a cable and his gaff could beach a walrus. He is a friendly fellow. I cannot tell his age as he is almost entirely hidden by knitted things – bobble hat, scarf, gloves, several jerseys – but he must be oldish as he tells me he is retired. I learn that he was a psychiatrist and shy away from him at once. I always have an uneasy feeling that psychiatrists will know that my brain is seething with lecherous thoughts or that I cannot concentrate on their conversation as my attention is riveted to the wart on the end of their nose.

I arrive at the three-masted ship. She was built in Whitehaven in 1888; then she was named the *Dunboyne*, now she is the *Af Chapman*. She looked fine from afar, she still has her spars, but nearby I see she is devoid of all her sails and much of her cordage – not surprising, she has not sailed for sixty-four years. She is dead, a hollow shell, a Sleeping Beauty no prince found to kiss. There is a gangway from the moorage, a sign by it says that the hulk is now a youth hostel. Two teenage girls emerge from a hatch and slope across the gangway. One is fattish with lank blonde hair, the other thin with fizzy blonde hair. They tell me that they are Danish.

'What's it like in there?' I ask.

'Cold, very cold, it freezes,' says Fizzy Hair. Lank Hair nods sadly.

'Comfortable?'

'It might be if it is not so cold. And paper sheets.' Another sad nod from Lank Hair.

'Is there a lot of room below?'

'A hundred and thirty-six beds, most of them empty.' Lank Hair nods even more sadly.

'They are divided into male and female parts.' Lank Hair is now too sad even to nod.

'But it is cheap,' adds Fizzy Hair, stoically.

'Ya, sheep,' nods Lank Hair, still sad.

I carry on along the shoreline. There are two other boats of interest: fore-and-aft schooners. One of the schooners is a three-master and the other two-masted with its foremast higher than the mainmast. (The biggest schooner ever built had seven masts, she was 5000 tons with an overall length of 385 feet and sank with all but one of the hands lost.)

I've come upon a very old cutter (single-masted, gaff rigged). My family owned one of these in the 1840s. She was a seventy-tonner called the *Ganymede*. My great-great-uncle Sam wrote: 'To sail her requires a crew of six sailors, captain, cook and steward, at say £10 [totally] a week. This Cutter is the best of her tonnage, in respect of cabins, of anything floating – but still wholly insufficient for a family party – in fact only a bachelor's boat.'

In another letter he began: 'I passed a sickish night at anchor.' It concluded: 'Oh dear I can't stay below any longer.' He sounds a bit unseamanlike compared with his father George, who crossed the Atlantic seven times, or his uncle Samuel, who crossed it even more as master of a slave trader.

As I ramble back toward my hotel I meet David Goldsmith, the embassy driver. 'I've got some spare time,' he says, 'I'll drive you back to the hotel and you can check out and then I'll show you some more ships.' So I pay my bill and David drives me to Mälardrottningen, 'The Queen of Lake Mälaren'. She is a clipper-bowed steam yacht of 1450 tons and 240 feet in length. Her twin screws are powered by a Krupp's diesel engine of 1800 bhp. She can carry 350 passengers and crew. She was built by Cox & Stevens in New York for C.K.G. Billings in 1924. Her name was then the *Vanadis*. In 1939 she was given to Barbara Hutton, the Woolworth's heiress, as an eighteenth birthday present. She was taken over by the

Royal Navy in 1940, her name was changed to *Warrior* and she served as an anti-submarine ship and then as an 'accommodation vessel' (does that mean a prison ship?), ending up in Panama. She then sailed under the ownership of a variety of Scandinavians, finally ending up here as an hotel (with fifty-nine rooms/cabins) and restaurant (for eighty diners). I pop in. As to be expected, it is a bit naff, with lots of mahogany and brass, a cosy 'Captain's Bar' and 'yo-ho-ho' type of announcements on cork notice boards. I get a price list: a cabin for one is about 800 kroner, the equivalent of £60, for twenty-four hours.

Next, David drives me to a wharfside where lines of working vessels are moored, mainly fishing boats converted to tripper cruisers. One boat is a mere hulk, just the beautifully crafted shell of a working boat. I pace her out — about twenty-five paces or seventy-five feet; she's a bit squat, so she's probably about the same tonnage if fully equipped and rigged. A tousle-headed man appears from below while I am doing the measuring. He is a Frenchman, Jean Raoul de Marcenne. He has been working on the hulk for about twenty years, doing it up: 'We'll soon be finished,' he says, optimistically. Her name is the *Áran*. She was built in 1903. She is a Baltic trader. I once sailed in a Baltic trader off the Turkish coast. My reaction to it was similar to that of great-great-uncle Sam's: being shallow-keeled, she rolled, as well as pitched, heaved, slewed, slid and yawed. The very words make me feel queasy.

V-adml. Cozumel Vireo

Villa Sallini
Roma

1995 ~ Tuscany.   All this sailing talk reminds me of the retired Italian admiral I met at a shooting party in Tuscany. He was immaculate in the best British tweeds and Italian leather, with an old-world courtesy and charm which made the girls a quarter of his age swoon with desire. His hawk-like profile recalled the origins of the term 'Roman nose'. He limped; he told me that his feet had never recovered from his days as a naval cadet aboard the *Leonardo da Vinci* where the punishment was to run up and down the ratlines (ladders) with bare feet.

Le Count Frederique di Francolin
> *(Freddy to his friends)*

Maintenance & Assistance
> *(A shoulder to cry on)*

TRUMP TOWER
Atlantic City

1998 ~ Atlantic City.   The Central Bus terminal in Lexington Avenue, New York, is a huge complex of skyscraper and glass and girders, like the bridge and superstructure of an aircraft carrier. I board the bus for the gambling city with twenty-three other passengers: fourteen black, five white, four Asiatic. The black ones look sad and are mostly women, oldish; the whites nondescript; the Asiatics are excited and chatter – so much for the 'inscrutable' oriental.

At ten o'clock the bus moves out of the murky basement to open daylight and heads south. We rumble between the skyscrapers and emerge into the shack-built suburbs, then further into townlets: the Stars and Stripes flutter everywhere, and are the only objects of any attraction. (The towns in this part of America are usually hideous.) Now we pass swampy land with reed beds, open pools where float Canada geese, the New Jersey turnpike, marshalling yards, granite outcrops, great boulders, an estuary, afar off a lovely bridge – as simple, elegant and basic as a snake's skeleton – lakes, ducks, a town of small factories and mills; in the far distance haze and smoke and standing cranes and derricks, pylons like dinosaurs wading across the marsh-lands, ships to seaward, a large eagle. Now we reach woodland; white weather-boarded houses under trees are cosy. After one and a half

[109]

hours, we are at the Forked River, where there are clumps of dead fir, burnt or drowned. We go through Smith Village – more trees – pass Pleasantville – more reeds. At last we are in sight of the city, a random line of dull skyscrapers, train yards, advertisements, shacks. A billboard proclaims

'WELCOME TO ATLANTIC CITY ~ AMERICA'S FAVOURITE PLAYGROUND'.

It stinks of sulphur. There is very little traffic. The pavements are almost completely bare of people. The place seems empty; London must have been like this in the time of the Great Plague. I disembus and tramp along a wooden walkway between a line of casino-skyscrapers and the sea. A strong wind sends sand stinging into my face.

As I enter the Trump casino I am given a free voucher for $19. Why have they given me this? I suppose Mr Trump thinks I am a sucker and that, having lost the $19, I will go berserk in my efforts to win it back. There is a huge hall full of the wailing of piped music and a strange twittering and plinking – the noise from the slot machines. Lights twinkle everywhere and are reflected off the polished brass sheets on the walls; chandeliers are festooned above, while heavy carpet sponges underfoot – all to give a touch of opulence. Most of the customers are women, late middle-aged. They sit in rows and are ceaselessly busy like old films of telephone-exchange girls. Some of them are working on three machines at a time. I get near one and the woman protects it like a hen with her clutch of eggs, cowering over it and hissing at me. Trays of free drinks are being borne by mini-skirted broads so you don't have to distract yourself away from the machines. A few people are eating in a café, open to the main hall so that they can be tantalised by the view of the action: the diners are shovelling their food down their throats as if they were stoking boilers; they want to get back to work.

Bored with wandering about, I put two $5 notes on a roulette table.

Ah, well, it was Trump's money, anyhow.

When I pop a coin into a machine, there are a lot of pleasing tinkles if it pays out; if nothing comes out, I sometimes feed it until it does.

'Good luck,' the machines often say, in creepy, unctuous voices, but what they are thinking is: 'Sucker, I am programmed to win.'

A coin is stuck. A push-button is near, to ring for help. An attendant hurries up. He is very tall, very thin, a coffin-shaped face framed by enormous ears, the lobes of which flap as he rummages in the entrails of the machine. 'Here,' he says, producing my 25 cent coin, 'you used the wrong thing, for this you need to buy special counters.' He tells me he is the second son of an Italian noble, that he used to fly his own private aeroplane taking tourists over Venice, that he was a big-game hunter in Liberia, had fought in Vietnam and has taken up his present job to learn the ropes before he sets up his own casino. He is very interesting but froths a bit at the mouth and I find his Geordie accent rather hard to understand. He was educated in England, he says; that is where he met his wife, the Countess Maureen. He gives me his card. It is quite merry, in contrast to his somewhat lugubrious demeanour.

Time to go. I empty my pockets to count my winnings.

I've lost $27 on the slot machines and $10 on roulette! That $19 was for a sucker after all. I've never liked that fellow Trump. He was frightfully nasty about the delightful Selina Scott.

1998 October ~ THE ARGENTINE, Buenos Aires

Having left Brazil this morning, I am now in the Argentine for the night, then off to Uruguay tomorrow.

I telephoned an Argentinian friend last week:

GC: I'm off to South America soon and I'll be in Buenos Aires for a long afternoon and short night, what is there interesting to do in those eighteen hours?

SYLVIA: I know the *very* thing. In the area of the old docks they have changed *masses* of the warehouses into night-clubs and bars specialising in the *tango*. You just pay to enter and you can tango *all night*.

GC: What an appalling idea. I cannot do the tango, and even if I could, I wouldn't want to, and even if I did want to, no-one else would want to dance it with me.

SYLVIA: Oh *everybody* would, they just *adore* blonds over there.
GC: How long has it been since we last met?

Now I am here I thought I'd go to the old docks anyway, I don't have to tango just to see what they have done. I am walking along a cobbled embankment with the water-filled docks to one side and the warehouses to the other. These are long brick buildings with lines of arched windows. Everything looks clean and scrubbed, artfully draped curtains frame tables laid for dinner, or bars with lines of bottles and glasses waiting for the evening. Yachts and motor boats are moored against the sides of the docks. In the distance I can see the three masts and two funnels of an old ship.

I am beside its bowsprit, which itself is as long as the mainmast of a large yacht. Below it the figurehead lies sprawled: a bare-breasted woman in a red liberty cap. Her plain face has a worried expression: with justification, she represents the Spirit of Argentinian Liberty. The ship's name is the somewhat cumbersome: *Fragata A.R.A. Presidente Sarmiento*. A notice by the gangway says she was built by Camell Laird of Scotland in 1897, that she is a cadet ship for the Argentinian navy, and that she is open to the public.

I board her and pay an entry fee to a sailor sitting behind a table. The decking stretches out fore and aft, the masts and rigging tower overhead, with the ratlines diminishing in size as they go up the masts. There is an extraordinary amount of weaponry all about, poking over the gunwales. It ranges from 120 mm cannons to the 37 mm rapid-fire Hotckiss with a pistol grip. The binnacle has the old-gold gleam of well-polished brass. I look to see in what direction the ship is pointing: 32° NE by N. The steerage is of three wheels on one spindle, big enough to have six men haul her about in adverse winds.

Below, there is a terrific smell of paint and engine oil. If sailing, I would be sea-sick within ten minutes. A mini-museum has been created: photographs on walls, objects in glass-fronted cabinets. The oddest of these is Lampazo, a stuffed dog of the big-and-shaggy variety, lying as if asleep. From my experience of dogs afloat, some wretched youth would have been commissioned ceaselessly to scrape its turds off the planking and hurl them overboard. Most of the other exhibits are of daily equipment from galley, cabin and berth, and officers' uniforms, mostly rather small. The wearers of these are shown in lines of photographs: maybe small in body, but huge in tufts, clumps, bristlings, fuzzments, droopings-down and sweepings-up of facial hair: moustaches, beards, side-whiskers, mutton-chops, Dundrearys, Newgate frills – everything, except, surprisingly, Bugger's Grips, those peculiar little tufts on the cheekbones favoured by certain British naval officers. Down eighteen brass steps into the engine rooms, divided up into cells, some of which hold the boilers, others fuel bunkers, yet others an incomprehensive jumble of valves and piping, and the long, narrowing tunnel above the keel which contains the propeller shaft. With the smell and heat and the motion it must be a nightmare down here in a storm. In beatific comparison, as I exit, I pass a lovely photograph of the ship running before the wind with her full suit of sail out, even the wing-like 'studding' sails attached to each side of the foresail and jutting far over the waves. (I once saw a ship like that. It was over forty years ago. I was halfway up a mountain beside the fjord-like Bay of Kotor, on the coast of Montenegro. It was an eerie, silent place; I was all alone. I looked down after a particularly difficult and steep scramble and saw below me a three-masted ship, her sails a billowing of clouds above the dark waters. She was so beautiful that I found my whole body shivering at the sight.) But for all her finery, the ship I'm aboard now is dying: there are signs of rot on the bridge and the strakes on one of the clinker-built lifeboats are warping.

Babu Soumitra Jacana B.A.

Sophisticated Guided Tours
— for the discerning

Block 4, Flat 33,
Chicana, Calcutta.

1983 ~ *Calcutta.* The Babu is stooping, bespectacled, earnest; he is wearing a well-pressed, frayed-at-the-edges suit. He is pointing out preliminary impressions of India as we drive to Calcutta. Firstly, and surprisingly, is the impression of greenness and lush growth: palm trees; small, rich fields; shrubbery, with lovely flowers (the pink of oleander, red of hibiscus and butter-yellow of frangipani); lagoons and ponds full of water hyacinths, their lilac flowers making a misty haze of colour over the vivid apple-green of the waxy leaves. Secondly, and of no surprise, is the dirt and dust, the squalor of the sprouting bustling striving communities, many of them Bangladeshi refugee camps: shacks walled with an assortment of planks, pales, posts and strakes, none of which seems to fit closely enough to stop eye-pryable gaps; an ocean of roofs, which, although predominantly a sort of pantile, are also of rags (old sacks, torn scraps of plastic sheeting, shreds of matting and just plain rags) strewn upon the roofs like unmade beds, sometimes held down by a haphazard arrangement of bricks and old tins and barrels tossed up in the hope that they would land in a useful place. The stench of the leather-tanning area is incredible: gaunt men stand up to their hips in steeping ponds of human excrement; on the banks of the sewerage lagoons are the leatherworkers' stinking, musty workshops; there is a flock of vultures by the verge. For the poor, scrawny cattle, my first (and continuous) wish is to give them worming pills. The Babu says there are forty thousand rickshaws, propelled either by bicycle riders or by thin-legged men toiling between shafts. Among the countless beggars, some have their hands or other bits and pieces of their bodies missing. People everywhere are selling, selling, selling (a ragged mat on a newspaper is laid out on the street, and a few tawdry articles are placed upon it, the vendor squatting with pitiful hope beside). The crowds increase as night falls. How young the people are, hardly anyone over thirty, and how few women. And how smart and prosperous the women look compared with the men. Is it because the sari is so elegant?

Amid our mini-bus load of people is an American couple, middle-aged, wearing huge hats and high-heeled boots of embossed leather. She is disapproving and sniffy of all she sees. He is rumbustious. 'Hey, Babu babe,' he says, 'what's that? – or this? or them? – or those?'

The Babu is getting increasingly peeved: 'I am not understanding this "babe" business. Please to take into consideration my maturity, and my educational credentials.'

'Anything you want, Babu, babe,' says the American cheerfully.

Jack Turnstone, F.R.S.L. M.J.
B. Lit.

'Teach and Tend'

c/o South London University
909, Gower Street
London

1989 ~ Havana.   I had the apt quote on the tip of my tongue, but could not remember it until too late, when he had gone. He was from a British charity, teaching English to Cuban children. We did not dislike each other, but disagreed on everything except how ghastly hot and muggy Havana was. He had a besotted admiration for Castro, citing 'Cruel necessity' for every unpleasantness I mentioned. What I was trying to remember was Pitt the Younger's remark: 'Necessity is the plea for every infringement of human freedom. It is the argument of tyrants; it is the creed of slaves.'

1998 October ~ CHILE, Santiago

Day 1.   I landed here from Uruguay in the morning. Our government has abetted the arrest of Pinochet, the former dictator of this country, which has enraged some Chileans. I was warned that my arrival and subsequent journey to our embassy might be 'difficult'. I could be made into a 'political pawn'. I was quite excited.

Disappointment. Nothing happened. I was met by one of our escorts – worried but stoic. I also had two escorts from some Chilean government organisation, attractive giggly girls who took me in the VIP mini-bus across the airport. We had a merry, non-politically-contentious conversation on the potential differences in the weather caused either by the masculine el Niño or the feminine la Niña. Does the weather have sex?

When we arrived at the embassy the crowds who had been throwing eggs and tomatoes had vanished. They were all having lunch on the pavement restaurants instead. Several waved ironically as I peered at them through the mini-bus windows. However, the morale in the embassy seemed low. No diplomat likes 'diplomatic immunity' to be treated in a cavalier fashion: the behaviour of the Iranians to the American diplomats resulted in the Iranians being the pariahs of the diplomatic world. Our fax machines have been churning out messages ranging from 'The Queen is a bitch and you are all children of bitches' to 'All last week your leaders were in China licking the bottoms of the murderers of Tien-an-men Square and Tibet. This week they find cause to . . .' Our staff have all liked the Chileans. The United Kingdom and Chile have been traditional friends. There is a sense of loss. My own Chilean friends are connected with the university and are thus generally anti-Pinochet, but even they seem to feel that his arrest, if merited, is a business of theirs and not of any other country.

Personally, I think he was an intolerable old tyrant, but he was opposed to another tyranny, even more brutal, whose politics were even worse, so a plague on all their houses.

I have been told to keep off the streets, as an unfortunate Australian and two Dutch were mistaken for Englishmen and beaten up.

Day 2. This evening I went out to dinner with Angélica and Daniéla. They took me to a Traditional Polynesian Restaurant. We were serenaded by a Traditional Polynesian Electric Organ accompanied by Traditional Polynesian Electric Guitars while Traditional Polynesian Damsels, mostly tall and blonde, wearing Traditional Coconut-shell brassières and grass skirts of plastic ribbons, hula-hulaed at us most beguilingly. When a waiter brought the menu round I asked if there was any missionary on it and he was not even remotely amused.

I ate freshwater crayfish followed by tunny fish steaks. While we ate, a smooth man in a dinner jacket came on to the stage and made some unfunny jokes and then called out the places where some of the diners had come from: 'a whole mini-bus full of our friends from Tokyo' (polite applause), 'Señor and Señora Palanque from Mexico' (more polite applause), 'the Florenzo Famillia from Sunny Spain!' (clap-clap), 'the gentleman over there – from England'. Our table burst into wild applause and clapping, as did another in the farther end of the room: otherwise it was all a chilly silence and critical staring or tactfully averted eyes.

Now, late at night, back in my hotel, I am wondering whether there will be any excitement when I leave tomorrow [Later: there wasn't – angry crowd all at football match.] Apparently Miss Evans, our ambassadress, has an ultimate weapon of defence: a signed photograph of Mrs Thatcher. She intends to lead the staff out of the burning embassy, holding it above her head, like a sacred icon.

Asio Otus
Lullula Arborea

Co-ordinators:
The Women's Rehabilitation Dept
Nigerian Ministry of Justice
Kiri Kiri Appapa
Lagos

1991 ~ Lagos. I can't sleep. I have been coming and going so much in the last few days I know neither the time nor date. I can't read, as the glare of

[117]

the bedside lamp makes my eyes sting and water. I cannot forget the sight of those wretched women hacking away in the broiling heat with mattocks, while the supervising men, official bullies, lounged about as idle as sloths.

Not Lullula, the only woman officer. She was not the tough nut I expected but a hugely built Mother Figure, charming, intelligent and kind. There was little she could do in helping the female ex-convicts into a better life except supervise the work imposed upon them; this she did with cheerful badinage rather than the officious shouting and strutting about of her male senior, the obnoxious Asio Otus. Seeing those wretched women this morning dominated by that tinpot tyrant reminded me of other male-female disparities I have seen around the world: for example the elegant women in saris toiling as rubble movers on the construction sites of Calcutta, while scruffy men fiddled with clods and pebbles beside them; the truculence of the Nigerian customs-men, the charm of the Thai Air stewardesses; the Ramboesque stamping and shouting and anxious sweating of Brazilian policemen at the scene of a mugging, the ice-cool efficiency of some Norwegian nurses dealing with a climbing accident on the Jotunheimens; the witty and attractive Asian women I used to do business with, the Chinese, Siamese and Indian wives of lazy scented slobs who idled about in their clubs. Even me: engrossed for twenty-five futile years in the construction and sale of bits of cloth, now a pepped-up postman idling in a luxury hotel, while my wife manages house, farm and estate and undertakes the most important thing which any human does and which only women can do – the rearing and basic education of the new generation. What are we men for? Are we going to become redundant? Men will degenerate. There will be nothing for us to do. Of the male/female task division between hunters and gatherers, the hunters are now superfluous. The final bastions, the hunting-shooting-fishing fraternities, are now under attack from urbanised, plasticised people who, at the best, do not understand and have no sympathy with the life, and at worst are motivated by social envy. The miner no longer need dig and delve, nor the broker negotiate and calculate: such things will be done by women with television screens and control panels, at home.

At present, in places, daughters are being murderously culled; eventually this practice will reverse and it will be recognised that boys are the ones dispensable, except for the fortunate few selected for stud purposes. And they will be chosen because of their effete, feminine traits. Eventually – the second virgin birth, then another, then men will be completely superfluous.

Well, odd how pessimistic moping makes one feel better.

FLORICAN AGENCIES
M. MAURICE FLORICAN

5, Tiberias Street	Piazza Vidi 12	Blvd Suchet 6780
Damascus	Roma	Paris
Syria	Italia	France

1974 ~ Damascus. Maurice was my Syrian agent when I worked for Courtaulds. He was a friend of a friend of a friend and I remain clueless about his background, except in remembering him as a Christian, as French in accent and attitude, as sophisticated, and, as a dedicated capitalist, stealthily cautious in socialist Syria. He was also hospitable:

'Damascus claims to be the world's oldest continuously inhabited city, old even for the Old Testament, invaded by Assyrians, Alexander the Great, Romans, Arabs, Mongolians, Turks, British; now the influence is French. I will show you around.'

We went to explore one of the most famous alleyways in the world, mentioned both in the Bible and the *Arabian Nights* as 'The Street which is called Straight'. The first length was fascinating and charming, private enterprise having still avoided the tyranny of the socialist oligarchy which runs the country. We walked through the long, tunnel-like arcade with its little booths and alcoves resounding with the noises of brass beaters and coppersmiths, radiating with the heat from the kilns of glass-blowers and of potters, smelling of the wares of the spice

[119]

merchants and purveyors of popcorn and pistachio nuts, and a-murmur
with the crooning beguilements of the merchants of silk and rayon, of
Pakistani gold and Bahraini pearls, of American cigarettes and Japanese
wristwatches, of myrrh, frankincense, second-hand books, mouse-
traps, swords, false eyelashes, rhinoceros horn cups and plastic sandals.
The arches and walls above our heads were sometimes built from
straight-edged blocks of stone, hewn by Roman masons, sometimes
they were a conglomeration of bricks and corrugated iron. The whole
shambles spans a period of time from the writings of the Old
Testament to the Thoughts of Henry Ford.

At the far end of the Street which is called Straight we saw a
bulldozer smashing down a millennium of human activity to make way
for office blocks.

The bulldozer was not the only example of European culture.
We drove past a vast, blank-faced building. It was grey and had
rows of tiny windows embedded into its walls. Maurice pointed to
it: 'The headquarters of Internal Security. We call it the Toe-nail
Factory.'

SAYAH ENTERPRISES & IMPORTERS

H. H. PRINCE SAYAH AL-COUGAL
44, NEW BLOCK BUILDINGS
RIYADH
SAUDI ARABIA

1976 ~ Riyadh. My 'contact-man' Reginald and I were met at Riyadh
airport by the car of the princeling who Reginald had chosen to be my
patron in the kingdom of Saudi Arabia.

My heart was low by the time we had reached Sayah's office: the heat
was debilitating; in spite of the money being spent on 'Civil and Urban
Refurbishment', the streets of the capital were litter-strewn and most of
the buildings were shoddily made and sand-stained.

The Arab way of running an office is to allow every one in: friends and relations, buyers and sellers, hunting and hawking companions, vendors of office equipment or of guns (together with their wares), pleaders for political favours and messengers carrying urgent and authoritative orders from mothers, wives, daughters, mothers-in-law and other unseen but influential womenfolk. I was ushered into the middle of this bedlam: it was centred on a huge sofa. Above this hovered a set of enormous smiling teeth, their snowy expanse accentuated by the glossy blackness of the beard around them: the general effect was of Popeye's enemy, Bluto, but Bluto wearing the simple robes of a desert Arab. They appeared simple only at the first glance; with a second glance I saw his keffiyeh had been lappet-woven on a 16-shaft dobby loom from 6-fold 84s cotton-count Sea-Island long-stapled, prime-harvested cotton, and that his cufflinks on his sleeves were cut from diamonds as big as thumbnails.

'Lay it on thick,' Reginald had advised.

'Good morning, your Highness, um . . . your Excellency . . . er . . . your . . .?'

'George,' he bellowed, 'welcome! And do not be so formal, there are six thousand princes and I am not among the important ones. I am what you might call "no great sheikhs".'

This was obviously an old joke, but well liked, for he fell about in helpless merriment and those in attendance tittered dutifully.

'And how is our friend, Harith Kahn? Still hunting, shooting and fornicating? He took me shooting to South Uist and he was the first chap they'd ever seen in a turban, and I was the first genoooine bedoooine.'

Sayah was an intelligent and shrewd man, which many of his fellow desert Arabs are, but he is also very hard-working, which many are not.

'I am just as Semitic and grasping as those chaps in Tel Aviv; but I like to let the visiting American and Japanese and French businessmen think that I am a poor little innocent from the desert. Then I con them. But we are still close to the nomadic life: the only difference between my grandfather and me is that he says "I hate that man because he

[121]

killed my camel" and I say "I hate that man because he burnt my Rolls Royce".'

He was a Welsh Nationalist: 'I was at Swansea University, and at weekends we undergraduates would march through the streets shouting: "Foreigners out – Foreigners out." And you English were the foreigners.'

The House of Commons

Mr James J. MacCaw, MP

1998 ~ London to Rome Flight.   I am sitting next to a newly elected MP who is an incompatible combination of the sleek and the burly. His suit is too tight: not of muscles, but because he has overindulged in subsidised food and drink. He thinks that as I am a Queen's Messenger I am obliged to listen to him; he may be right, so I am. He talks enthusiastically about himself. His enthusiasm is not infectious. He talks sometimes of 'we workers' and does not include me in this classification. I have been paid to work as a spinner, weaver and dyer, and have worked unpaid as a shepherd, groom, forester and rat-catcher. Turns out that he was a solicitor.

1998 October ~ BRAZIL, São Paolo

Day 3.   Here last night and this morning, on my way back to London. It is sunny; there are a few clouds and a cooling wind of about 15° C.

This is not a happy city: the second largest built-up area in South America, officially with ten million people but with the population growing uncontrollably every minute, in spite of the appalling ravages of AIDS.

I have a couple of hours to spare: time to walk up the main drag, the Avenida Paulista. The pavement is of the typical Latin American black and white cobbling, set in designs of squares, zigzags or undulations. To either side are modern skyscrapers. Unlike New York, where the narrow streets give one the sensation of walking down the bottom of canyons, this road is sixty paces wide so that one can see the buildings in their entirety. Most are nondescript, but there seems to be a local speciality, the roof aerial. Some are small Eiffel Towers, or like spindly oil-rigs; some are attractive with web-like complexities; some are disks; some are like the skeletons of dead pine trees, or have rows of spikes like the spine of a fish. I think they may be part of a Keep-up-with-the-Joneses syndrome. Amid the cement monoliths there are a few – very, very few – of the old houses left. They are small and white and covered with ornamental plasterwork as ornate as the icing on a wedding cake, similar to the coral-built houses of Havana. They crouch, small and old and overdressed and unhappy, like pensioners at a pop concert. There are trees: palms, banyan, the purple iopoxa. But the overall impression is of urbanisation for league after league. I hear a bird singing in a tree. I cannot see it. Perhaps it is a recording, man has destroyed nature here so has to imitate it: cliffs of bare rock have been replaced by cement walls; rain and wind are now the ceaseless dripping from faulty air-conditioning and the gusts of air from opened doors; the scents wafting from hairdressers replace those of wild flowers; instead of the blowzy smell of rotting vegetation there is the stink from a fast-food shop; instead of leaves and dead branches the litter is of scraps of plastic and paper; a sudden roar, not a wild beast, but the metro passing beneath my feet.

The people are small and dark; the men are squat, while many of the women are willowy. Some of them wear complicated teeth-bracing like American girls half their age. Is this another sign of 'one-upmanship'?

Oh, oh, I should have learnt by now and remembered the New York maxim: 'Never look a weirdo in the eye.' He sidles up. Old, bent and shabby, he has thin wisps of hair on a yellow-blotched scalp; his eyes are pale blue – unusual here – and his teeth are horrible. Is he smiling or snarling? He says nothing, just stares.

[123]

I'm going to strangle this little blighter soon, if he doesn't push off. He's been following me now for about quarter of an hour: he doesn't speak, doesn't get in the way, doesn't pluck imploringly at my sleeve, just stares. I now know what a gnu in a safari park feels like. It's more irritating, even alarming, than if he was showing hostility. Are my flies done up? Yes. Have I dribbled something large and strange on my tie? No, not any more than usual. Is my shirt-tail hanging out? What's so interesting about me? I stop to inspect my reflection in a shop window. He stops, stands beside me and stares at what I am staring at.

He has disappeared after I darted across the road just as the traffic lights were changing. After ten minutes I have to recross the road to get back to my hotel – and he's here! Rumpelstiltskin is waiting for me, grinning with the horrible friendliness of a skull.

'Good morning,' he says (his voice is unexpectedly deep, with a lilt in his accent; he is evidently not a local). 'I know you.'

'We've never met.'

'I know what you are.'

'?'

'So tell him, will you?

'Tell who? Tell who what?'

'Tell him I'm dead. He'll know who he is.'

'But I don't! Who is he? And who are you?'

But he's gone.

I return to my hotel room. After the nasty experience that Steven had in Lagos when, naked, he drew back the shower curtain and found four naked prostitutes behind it, I always look behind the shower curtain when I enter my bathroom. No sinister little man. Perhaps he really was dead.

Mr & Mrs Edward Phalarope

Quinta da Marsala
Funchal
Madeira

1953 ~ Madeira.   This Portuguese-owned island in the Atlantic, almost 360 miles from the African coast, is about thirty miles by ten. Pico Ruivo, the highest peak, in the middle of the island, is 6106 feet. Much of the rugged basaltic upland ends abruptly at the sea in the form of precipices, the biggest sea-cliff, Cabo Girao, is nearly 2000 feet high. It is a pleasant, healthy place, warm enough to grow bananas and avocados at sea level, but never stuffy because of the sea breezes; and the inland mountains are impressive and beautiful. It is famous for its embroidery and its wine. As Ogden Nash wrote:

Madeira is the home of wineries,
And extremely expensive embroidered fineries.
I seem to sense a relation tender
Between vintner and embroidery vendor.
Free sample sippings of the grape
Inflate the tourist to a shape
In which, by the time he's embroiled in the embroidery
    imbroglio
He will pay for a dozen doilies for the price of an authentic
    First Folio.

The Madeiran wine trade was given its greatest boost as a result of a British ordinance of 1663 declaring that 'Madeiran wine . . . may be carried thence to any of the lands, islands, plantations, colonies, territories or places to His Majesty belonging, in Asia, Africa or America, in English built ships.' At that time the English colonies were forbidden wine from France, Italy, Spain and Portugal, so the Madeirans were virtually given the monopoly of wine to the British Empire and the fleet. A few families still have a tradition of having Madeira rather than port as an after-dinner wine. During the wars of Queen Anne's reign, our ships often found it difficult to call at Madeira and so surplus stocks of wine accumulated; this was distilled into 'brandies' which were later used to fortify some of the better wines. Some of the English families which moved to Madeira to export the wine still live there, and are still involved in the trade. Among these are the Phalaropes.

Edward Phalarope had lent Dominie and me one of his spare villas for our honeymoon. It was on the hill overlooking Funchal, the bougainvillaea- and wisteria-draped capital of Madeira.

The people of Madeira were charming and most hospitable. We ate and drank enormous quantities in their houses, and the butler was kept busy organising our return hospitalities. Some of the people were pleasantly eccentric, old Mrs B***, for example, did not like autumn, so every year, at the end of summer, she had her gardeners go up the trees in her twenty-five-acre garden and pick off the leaves. Next morning it was winter. So we were told.

There used to be only a few wheeled vehicles in Madeira; loads were dragged over the slippery cobbles of the streets in ox-drawn sledges. If the loads were passengers, the sledges were furnished like little rooms, with curtains. Another way of getting about was by hammock; it was slung on a pole and carried at each end by an unfortunate peasant. Edward liked to go shooting in the volcanic mountains in the centre of the island; it was rumoured that the bearers had finally rebelled after the third time he had inadvertently shot off the head of a front bearer.

We went shark fishing with him. They were hammerheads, lured from the Pacific by the offal thrown from the Norwegian whalers returning home. Our boat was relatively small: the dorsal fins of the sharks looked like the sails of enemy submarines as they glided past; when the sharks swam under us they turned over so we saw the pale turquoise-blue of their under-parts, and the sickle shape of the down-turned mouths, and the extraordinary eyes far apart on the grossly misshapen heads, more like space monsters than anything from this earth. We caught none, but one of them snapped a rod as thick as my wrist.

One day he took us up into the mountains. We left the cosy, almost Mediterranean coastal villages and climbed up into the mist-shrouded heights. There were deep ravines and jagged peaks, some with the remnants of snow upon them. Hydrangeas were in full flower by the roadsides, their blossoms pale-blue globes the size of human heads. There was a scent of pine and eucalyptus. We came upon a small village. The villagers were busily at work, the men tilling their terraced fields or weaving wickerwork, the women making Madeira lace. This is mainly of linen fabrics, napery and bedding, the openwork designs being emphasised by the brown embroidery at the edges. Dominie bought a tablecloth. We still use it on the rare occasions we need one; normally we eat off the scrubbed kitchen table or the polished dining-room one.

Another friend, also a shipper, gave us a bottle of 1801 Malmsey (Madeira, unlike port, can be kept almost indefinitely).

On our return from honeymoon, Dominie and I went to live in a bungalow in Derbyshire, near the factory whose floor I was learning to sweep. After a month, our first guests came to stay the weekend. Once you are married, you become middle-aged, and Dominie and I scurried about doing middle-aged things: Dominie in the kitchen, stirring and tasting and roasting; me in the garden, weeding, watering, mowing and pruning.

'This is very good pudding, what is it?' said Henry Grousebutt.

'It's called zabaglione, it's made out of white of egg and sugar and Madeira,' replied Dominie.

A horrid thought assailed me. When dinner was over I sneaked off to the cupboard where I kept the drinks. The Malmsey was no longer there.

Still, it was very good pudding, and we were only just married, and anyhow we've got a tablecloth and Henrietta as a memento of our honeymoon.

Marie Eloise Jacamar

EXQUISITES

Ottawa   Washington   Paris   New York

1999 ~ New York. The businesswoman I sat next to at breakfast could be any age in the 'middle-aged' class for, like the things she sells, she is beautifully preserved, polished, painted and regilded: she wears an immaculate suit; her hairstyle is carved out of mahogany, while her face and hands are of the most flawless ivory, teeth as white and even as the keys on a piano; I notice a wedding ring; she is handsome rather than pretty.

We had a slightly embarrassing start: I was put at the table next to hers and decided to eat looking out of the window; she had decided to sit looking into the room. As we were so close we could not but help notice each other nibbling and sipping and mopping up the runny eggs. Absent-mindedly I was licking clean the little foil container which had held my marmalade when I caught her rather reproving eye.

'Er, it's not that I'm starving,' I apologised, 'it's just that I have not got my pen.'

'That explains it all,' she replied.

'What I mean is that I like the name of my marmalade, Smuckers, and need to take the label to my notebook, to write it down. I'll forget it, otherwise, you see.'

'Smuckers is a perfectly good name, like your "Robinsons",' she said.

'So you know England?'

It appears that she owns four 'bijou' art shops, one of them here. She specialises in 'objects of virtu' – little gilded Buddhist and Hindu idols, French clocks, English snuffboxes, Chinese jades, Persian miniatures; Lalique, Fabergé, Lafitte and so on.

She always has breakfast here to relax; her husband stays behind to keep shop. From her brief description of him, he sounds rather wet.

She told me she is Canadian. I told her I had been in Ottawa the day before: bitterly cold, $-20°$ C. This was the first time I had been met by a snow plough. A huge scraper blade had been bolted on to the truck which met me: you can change the angle and height with controls inside the truck.

She told me that another ingenious attachment for Canadian vehicles is a whistle on the front bumper: when the car gets up a bit of speed the whistle emits a supersonic screech which frightens away any beaver, moose or Mountie wandering about on the road.

Shua Tinamou
Director/Journalist
MONGOLIA TV

Ulaan Baatar

1998 ~ *Ulaan Baatar.* I emerged from the mists of infancy into the clarity of childhood when snow was on the ground – and so I always feel young in the cold and the snow. I exult at the first sight of Mongolia in winter: the iced-up rivers and tarns, the patches of white in the folds of the mountainsides, the people stumping along in the long dressing-gown-like dells and heavy felt wellington boots; everything made extra vivid in an atmosphere as clear and sharp as glass.

I had dinner with some Mongolian friends during my last visit: not in the cosy, smuggy, smoky confines of a ger, but in a tiny flat in one of the Russian-built apartment blocks, already cracking and flaking after four years. One of the other guests was their television friend who had filmed my house and estate to show Mongolian viewers an example of an English house and farm. The Mongolians, being shepherds, would be specially interested in Jake, the sheepdog: the Mongolians do not use dogs for herding, just for protection against wolves and lynx and snow leopard. Unfortunately Jake is an uncommonly inept sheepdog, so I had to make it up as we went along: 'You see how the dog has deliberately separated the flock into seven different groups, how he is driving them away from us at a fast gallop, how he is circling round that little bunch to take them towards the river. Ah, he's got one down and feeling her leg to see if she is fat enough for market.'

They also filmed me pointing things out in my house – furniture and pictures and such-like. What seemed to interest the cameraman particularly were the log baskets, full of logs, but he said what interested him most was how many things we possessed had been inherited – passed down from previous generations: 'We have inherited nothing from our ancestors, the communists took everything away.'

1998 November ~ ISRAEL, The Judaean Desert

Looking for a suitable place for a hermitage is not dissimilar to finding a decent place to pitch a tent. The hermit seeks a site in a remote spot: nobody for miles; almost inaccessible – a cave halfway up a cliff or on top of a pinnacle or on a deserted island; he unrolls his bedding, lights a fire, brews himself a cuppa, says his prayers, snuggles down to sleep – in the morning he wakes up and finds all the neighbouring caves full of other hermits. A *laura* (a community of individual but centralised cells) has appeared. In any group of people there is always a busybody who wants to start ordering the others about, or who decides a bit of 'community spirit' is needed. This Bossiest Hermit disguises his ambitions by organising a committee and working through that. He then starts to unify and centralise: a chapel will be built, followed by a communal kitchen and refectory; then visitors will arrive to praise, pray or plead and a dormitory will be made for them; then the extra costs will have to be paid for so the other hermits will be set to work writing manuscripts and weaving baskets and squeezing olives and selling scented candles and liqueurs; then the original hermit will die and he will be canonised as St Anonymous the Testy and his bones will be set in gold and garnets for the adoration of pilgrims. The whole site has developed into a monastery, situated in the most inconvenient place possible, conglomerated around the original cave: inconvenient, but picturesque.

The Judaean desert had many of these. The majority of the desert stretches between Jerusalem and the Dead Sea. The land ranges from the hummocky to the mountainous, sometimes gouged out by flash-streams into deep wadis, sometimes with cliffs which mark previous courses of long-gone rivers or levels of the still-shrinking Dead Sea; it is gritty and arid, better suited to goats than sheep – a place for the nomadic or the ascetic.

The desert was at its busiest in the period between the confirmation of Christianity as the religion of Byzantium in 313 until the Muslim Conquest of the seventh century. Officially approved, so unable to suffer the joys of martyrdom, Christians, instead, swarmed into this most inhospitable of places and founded a multitude of churches and at least seventy-three monastic settlements. Only a very few of these remain. One of the most dramatically situated of them is that of St George of Koziba. I have decided to visit it in the spare time I have today.

Both our usual embassy drivers are away on a 'Protective Driving' course. Today's temporary driver from our embassy in Tel Aviv to our consulate in Jerusalem is called Joe. He is young, Israeli-born; one of his parents is Russian, the other Polish. It should make an interesting mixture, but he is surly and scowls when told that I could have the use of him and his car for the next four hours. We drive away from the consulate with Joe grumbling about Abdul, our charming and sophisticated Palestinian security officer.

'Always complaining, never happy or grateful, these Arabs.'

'You must sympathise with Abdul, his ancestors toiled over his little vineyard for centuries, now his inheritance has been taken from him with some bureaucratic excuse.'

Like many men whose ancestors did nothing worth inheriting, Joe has a dislike of inheritance. He would find himself at home in today's House of Commons.

'No-one wanted his grapes, it is better to be a good bypass for the new housing community. These Arabs, they're living on nothing but goat meat and dates until we showed them what to do.'

'Maybe, but the Arabs have a saying that "it is better to eat one's own weeds than another man's wheat".'

Joe grunts and I shut up. It is stupid to get involved in other people's wars, and the war in Palestine/Israel is a civil war between neighbouring Semitic peoples. Like all civil wars, both sides have justification for hatreds and many excuses for their eternal vendettas.

We are about ten miles from the Dead Sea; in following the faint lines on my small map we are driving up a track above the Wadi Qelt. The track is unmetalled: the surface is merely rubble, with traces of the footprints of numerous small hoofs.

We drive past a bedouin camp: shacks covered with sacking, tents, broken down trucks, a brushwood compound full of sheep; goats stray among the untidiness; children and a few women stare at us.

'We may be going the wrong direction. Perhaps that woman can tell us the way,' Joe says.

Strange, despite living next to Arabs for thirty years, Joe does not know them.

'Joe, for God's sake do not talk to her. If any man sees us talking to their women we'll be lynched.'

We pass more encampments. In one I see an extraordinary beast with huge grey antlers; on second sight it turns out to be a white donkey tethered to a dead tree, the branches of which seem to be sprouting from its head.

Joe is getting nervous. 'Two Israelis are killed near here last month,' he frets, 'if I am saying to another Israeli I am being here he is saying I am mad.'

His apprehension seems to be contagious, even his car has become fearful: it creeps nervously round corners, then if it sees a bedouin tent it gives a little jump, it shies away from a man on a donkey, it scuttles past an encampment, it gets slightly stuck and stalls in fright; revived, after some nervous coughing, it scrabbles in the rubble of the track and then rushes off in relief.

We come to a hillock beside the track which has a crucifix on the top of it.

'I'll go up there and look at the view and see if the monastery is in sight,' I tell Joe.

As I approach the cross I see that there is an Arab with a carpet laid out, upon which he has arrayed some silver jewellery, some leatherwork and a row of toy sheep. A camel lounges nearby, sitting on legs folded up like a collapsed deck-chair. Another Arab leaps to his feet and hurries towards the car. He'll probably tell Joe he is the car park attendant and wants a fee. When I reach the cross I see that I am on the edge of a deep ravine. And there is the monastery, halfway up the cliff on the other side. To the left of it there is a waterfall, a wonderful sight in this arid waste. There is a belt of lush growth to either side of it, nourished by the spray. I cannot see the bottom of the wadi, but the area just below the monastery is also lush, a garden-cum-oasis with date palms, cypresses and olive trees. The walls of the monastery rear from it as if hewn from the face of the cliff. From my position above it I can look down and see a complexity of walls and enclosures. The buildings are of the same pinky-beige colour as the surrounding rock but the window and door frames have been painted white; it is all dominated by bright blue domes.

The cataract, and the monastery asleep in the sun counteract with the starkness of the surroundings: the arid mountains, the apparently fathomless gorge. This, according to legend, is the place where Elijah lived for three and a half years, being fed by ravens, and where Joachim hid for forty days to mourn the barrenness of his wife until told by an angel to stop fretting as they were to be the parents of a girl who would become the Madonna, the mother of the Messiah.

As I gaze down, I see only one sign of movement: a languid furling and unfurling of a flag, the red crusader's cross on a white background – the flag of St George. Actually, that is somewhat irrelevant as the St George who founded this monastery was a Cypriot monk, born around AD 550, not our patron saint who was probably a Palestinian Arab, martyred around AD 300.

'That is the flag of St George,' I tell Joe, who has arrived with the other Arab.

'Yes,' says the Arab, pointing to the monastery, 'St George.'

I point to myself, 'I am George too.'

The Arabs are suitably impressed: 'Perfidious infidel,' they think.

'What is the name of your camel?' I ask the first Arab.

'It is Sayad.'

'What does that mean?'

He points to the sky and shrugs and smiles and says: 'Nice day . . . lucky . . . good.' One can take one's pick.

According to the Arabs, to get to the monastery Joe will have to drive to the end of the wadi and I will then have to walk: forty minutes there, forty minutes to explore, forty minutes back, forty minutes to get lost; I may not have the time so I tell Joe to drive on to Jericho, about ten miles away.

We pass a sign which says 'Sea level' and continue downhill. My ears pop with the increasing pressure. Actually, ears 'pop' if one is ascending; they must be doing the opposite at present. What is the opposite of pop? I experiment aloud: 'Pip – bip – bup – hub – gob – gug? That's it, gug! gug – gug. Yes, definitely, gug'.

Joe is staring at me from the corner of his eyes.

The Dead Sea, at 1300 feet below sea level, is the lowest natural point on the earth's surface. I have seen it in many colours, the most typical of them being metallic: molten steel, polished silver, mercury, lead, cast iron, zinc. Today it is softer: a Cambridge blue which hazes to nothing in the far distance.

We approach Jericho: the outlying holdings are of banana groves, palm trees, a field of maize, another full of big leaves and yellow flowers – a vegetable of the marrow/melon/cucumber family. Here is a huge new building: a casino, 'The Oasis'. For some subconscious puritan reason I am rather shocked but Joe says: 'It is good, one of the few places where Israelis and Arabs are getting together and agreeing that they all are having the bad lucks.' It is owned by Austrian Jews.

I want to see the changes in Jericho since I was last here six years ago. We potter about. Jericho has become seedy with scruffy streets, trashy new buildings and crumbling old ones, military areas fenced off with barbed wire, out-of-work people hanging about, looking sour. We stop at an Arab-owned grocer's and I buy three kilos of a small (and delicious) avocado pear for 24 shekels (£4). It always strikes me as odd that the currency of Abraham and Solomon and even Judas should be used for such mundane purposes as the purchase of fruit and veg.

We stop for lunch at a roadside eater. We sit in the veranda, shaded by an awning, and drink bottled grapefruit juice and eat balls of fried chickpeas called falafel, chunks of roasted gristle which is either goat or mutton, small stewed onions which I think excellent after I realise that they are not eyeballs, fried aubergine, some rabbit-foody salad of mixed leaves, all of this with boiled rice, and bread of the size, shape, smell and texture of the sole of a bedouin's sandal.

Deciding that there is not much more to see of Jericho, we leave. From the outskirts, looking over salt flats towards the sea, I see a square block of a building surmounted by a silver dome. I look it up in my guide book, the best of them all for any information archaeological and historical: *The Holy Land*, by Jerome Murphy-O'Connor, OP. He identifies the building to be, like St George's of Koziba, a Greek Orthodox monastery. This one is dedicated to St Gerasimus, who founded a *laura* here in AD 455. The monastery was created from the presence of the *laura* of seventy hermitages, some of which, cut into rock, still survive. After the founder saint died in 475 the monastery declined; in 1185, when the Byzantine traveller, pilgrim and author John Phocas visited here, he found it all ruined, with only one hermit, living alone but for two pet lions.

There is a car park – empty – beside the monastery. Joe sits in the car while I walk up a shady alley between the stone walls of the monastery and an oasis-garden of palm, banana and oleander, through a tunnel-like main entrance into a small and cosy yard, stone flagged, with a stairway against one wall and overlooking galleries on the other three. There is a well in the centre; trees shade the flagging and birds murmur and twitter in cages hung from the branches. A chapel to one side is cool and lit by night-lights which flicker in glass bowls. The barrel-vaulted ceiling is painted and gilded; with hooded, sleepy eyes, icons gaze at me in the half-light; there is a large mural of a very pretty Madonna wearing a golden crown and, with a torpedo-shaped breast, suckling the infant Christ. I peer into the top of a glass-fronted cabinet and suddenly realise that the round grey objects are not ostrich eggs, but skulls. A pile of teeth is in one corner, and jaw bones have been arranged into a pretty pattern. In the compartment below, the bones are stacked in order of type: neatly, the femurs and ribs; in tangled heaps, the vertebrae and knuckle bones. I re-enter the courtyard and see a partly open door opposite. As I peep through it a surly hairy hag of a woman barges me out of the way and slams it shut in my face. She has a thin slit of a mouth, as if some cook has tested a suet dumpling with a knife-prod; eyes like mildewed raisins; hair like the pubic fuzz of a camel. I expect she has something to do with the monks' penance: 'Right, Brother Amos, at your solitary vice again. Five hundred lashes and two weeks on your knees in prayer and fasting; alternatively five minutes in bed with our Mildred here.'

I go back to the car and tell Joe that my guide book says that there are some hermits' cells nearby: 'Follow the security road running due east from the monastery for about a kilometre until it rises to a rusting tank in a fixed position. To the left is a grove of palm trees. The caves are in the steep cliff-face.'

We drive along a track, Joe fussing about his tyres, his sump, the dust, the Arabs and getting lost. We pass the tank: not a water container, but the burnt-out hulk of a Jordanian (I think) Sherman. We carry on, alongside a crude barbed-wire fence.

'There is a minefield on the other side of this wire, you will see warning signs with skulls painted on them.'

We come upon one of these signs, but its back is towards us.

'Oh Moses! It's the minefield that we are in!'

'Don't worry,' I soothe, 'look, the ground is covered with hoof marks, most of the mines must have exploded by now.' Nevertheless, it is somewhat gingerly that I tiptoe among the goat tracks and lift the wire to let the car sneak under.

We must have overshot our destination. Joe turns the car round, shuttling to and fro, gaining an inch a time, terrified lest his wheels should go over the edge of the track. I see a little grove of palms below an escarpment. Joe parks the car and I start to walk along the edge of the cliff. It is made of layers of a whitish accretion. I suppose this was once the bed of the Dead Sea – it has dropped 750 feet over the last 50,000 years. I wonder if it is still salty: I break off a bit of the rock and nibble. Yes, a salty tang, and a bit fizzy. I round a corner and Joe disappears from view, the last I see of him is his worried face staring at me through the windscreen.

The palms are a miserable lot: many have fallen, others are ring-barked, or have snapped. There are tufts of a spiny bush; a covey of half a dozen red-legged sand-partridges starts up; a beautiful bird lands on a stump and looks at me. It is long and elegant, basically white with a long black side-stripe from tip to tail and a yellow patch below; it is a grey wagtail. Another covey of partridges bursts from under my feet. The hermits' cells are above me, merely rectangular entrances cut into the rock. They never had any doors 'in perfect conformity with the ruling of Gerasimus that members of the *laura* should leave their cells open'. One of the cells is a chapel. They are linked by a walkway cut in the rock, a mere ledge. I cannot get up, there is no way; my book says that the entry is from above, but 'only to be attempted by the agile'. I am wearing my Queen's Messenger clothes, the only kit I have in the country, so cannot risk getting filthy.

I zigzag between the bushes and palms back to my car.

'Why is it that rocks you are eating?' is Joe's first remark.

'To see what they taste like, of course.'

He makes no comment, but starts the car, gets into first gear and we are off on our return journey to Jerusalem.

ARCHITEKT

PROFESSOR LUDVIG VON EIDER

WIEN

1988 ~ Amman. I met this charming old donnish Austrian at a hotel in Jordan. His suit was as crumpled as his face; his specs were held together by a bit of sticking plaster; his fingernails were remarkably dirty and broken. He was in the country supervising an archaeological dig. I told him I had recently become greatly admiring of Herod the Great, in spite of his bad press over the Slaughter of the Innocents: Herod was a wit, a great orator, a skilful politician, an athlete, attractive to women (including Cleopatra), a builder of magnificent constructions. While thus enthusing I wondered: 'What happened to Salome, the Dancer? She's had a bad press too, but it was her mother, also Salome, who was the really poisonous one.'

He told me something which has pleased me ever since: Salome married several times (it was spread about by the sour-faced old hermits that her insatiable lusts wore out her husbands) and she finally ended up as the Queen of Lower Armenia. She died while skating: she fell through the ice and the returning floes sliced her head off.

'Ah-ha!' said all the Christians smugly. 'Told you so. Serves her jolly well right!'

What interests me was that she went skating. It seems such an ordinary-extraordinary thing for her to have done.

| PAOLO FLAMINGO
Presidente – VISCOSITA

Isla d'Ostragot – VENEZIA | RACHAEL GOLDFINCH

Palazzo Vermicelli
Venezia | *Contessa di Minivet*

Palazzo Palagineria

Venezia |

1960 ~ Venice.   The old Contessa Minivet was a true Venetian and had the sexy lisp and fair skin of her fellow citizens, but by the time I met her, age had wrinkled and wizened her into a hunch-backed chimpanzee – nevertheless a beautifully dressed one. Like many local aristocrats she was almost penniless, but she had a 'protector' who kept her in the way to which she had been accustomed. Paolo Flamingo, the Protector, was also a Venetian; his father had been the Minivet family's Major-domo. He was large, bald and pallid-fleshed and was always immaculately dressed in a double-breasted suit, no matter how hot the weather. He looked rather like Chas. Addams's 'Uncle Fester'. He had made millions with a combination of shrewdness, hard work and Mafia-type tactics – and, possibly, contacts. When he became very rich he used his fortune to emulate the Venetian merchant princes of earlier centuries.

As the partridges on the mainland near Venice congregate every St Valentine's Day, to celebrate the start of a new breeding season, so, on the same day, would the old Contessa hold a party in her palazzo on the Grand Canal. We were asked to the great event. We were taken from the Danieli Hotel to the palace in the Contessa's private gondola. It was like a black swan, with a long arched neck and a keeled prow that clove the oily darkness of the canal. The gondolier wore the Contessa's colours in his hat; a train of sable velvet trailed in the water behind us; bewigged and liveried footmen helped us land. The old Contessa, bejewelled and haughty, received us at the top of the staircase where she preened and strutted as proud as a peacock.

She had peacocks in the garden. They would pace solemnly between the lines of miniature box, sip fastidiously from the alabaster shell below the tiny fountain, peer imperiously from the stone convolutions of the gazebo then, if disturbed, swear and screech like fishwives.

We knew the Venetians because of their associations in my father's business, the textile trade. One of Flamingo's successful schemes was to make rayon from a local product. Rayon is not a 'synthetic' fibre like nylon, which is an oil-based plastic; rayon is a 'man-made' fibre, made out of cellulose, the natural skeleton of most plants. In its pure natural form it can be seen as cotton or flax, it can be extracted from plants such as trees or straw, melted down, and re-solidified into filaments and fibres. The raw material that Flamingo used was the reed which grows in huge quantities in the swamps and lagoons around Venice. He had used some of his profits to build an extraordinary little village for his workpeople on the banks of the Venetian Lagoon. We toured it: each cottage was like a miniature doll's house; gardens were tended in front of each one (by company gardeners, no-one was expected to ruin any conformity by individual planting or tending); there were fountains at each crossroads. It also had a school, church and hospital.

Rachael Goldfinch was an American, not a Venetian, but she too had a palace. A friend of a friend, she invited us to visit her one evening. The most noticeable thing we saw as we walked through the twilit garden was a large modernistic bronze statue of horse and rider. The rider was obviously and excitedly male, his enormously erect equipment was a gleaming gold in comparison to the dark bronze of the rest of the statue. Miss Goldfinch joined us looking at it. 'There's this Venetian guy,' she explained, 'once a week he swims over the canal, with a can of polish between his teeth, climbs over the wall, and polishes that bit of this statue. We've got used to it.'

The interior of the palazzo was entirely in white: carpeting, walling, upholstery, and eight white dogs of the small and yapping variety. The pictures on the walls stood out in intense and vivid comparison. Some, particularly the Picassos, Matisses and Klees I saw with a shock of recognition; others were quite frightful. Miss Goldfinch had a penchant for young artists whose abilities were not always on the artistic side.

She was, to my adolescent mind, extraordinarily ugly: her head, as round as a football, with heavy, creased, battered features, startlingly similar to those of Sid James, but apparently she was attractive and she was never short of men. 'I just love England,' she told me, '*three* of my husbands were English, you know.'

It is autumn now, many years later. Venice has changed: she was often willing to sell herself, as a mercenary or a courtesan to any soldier or trader who came soliciting favours but now, like an old tart, she can't afford to be fussy. Japanese strew corn on the flagstones, so they may photograph each other feeding the birds. British tourists try on silly gondolier's boaters and squeal with merriment. The French scowl, the Americans gawp, the Germans look suspicious and the Nordics clump about with huge rucksacks as if they were about to go mountain climbing rather than shop for blown-glass goblets. The gulls in the lagoon choke on the French letters which float on the foul waters. Pollution is poisoning the place. It always stank: wet mud and sewerage, but to those smells are added the rancid stinks of fish and chips with vinegar, hot dogs with mustard, popcorn and pizzas. Guano bedaubs the statues and urns that ornament the buildings bordering the great square, graffiti deface the walls: 'Mario y Karen', 'Up the Wolves', 'A bas les juifs', 'shit'. In the piazzas pigeons still patter and pout, familiar denizens of Venice, but they are being jostled and harassed by squabbling hordes of sparrows, imported by cargo ship and passenger liner.

As the migrating swallows fly over Venice, so did the androgynists flock here for their autumn reunion in the piazzas and alleyways below. Each year there are fewer and fewer, both the swallows and the 'exquisites'; they are both vanishing species, being replaced by more vigorous, brasher types. The old men wander the flagged ways, their age and inclination giving them a short-stepped, mincing little gait. They are immaculate in plumage of silk and Sea-Island cotton and kidskin, from fringed scarf to polished shoes, with a pair of gloves held in one hand and a cane or pencil-thin umbrella in the other. Some of them have the lightest of powders on their cheeks, and discreet pearl-tinted polish on their fingernails. They look askance at the moustached Rambos loping by, their steps made springy by air-soled trainers, their beefy hands entwined, their tight-arsed jeans and 'Gay Power' T-shirts.

But here and there you see a Venetian: a wispy nun, a burly workman, a man in a striped jersey who comes up and whispers 'Gondola, gondola?', as if he were a pimp peddling an exotically named whore.

It is all gone now. Rachael Goldfinch is dead, her palazzo is a museum. The Contessa is also dead, plaster is flaking off leprously from the palace walls, stagnant water slops idly on the mossy steps which lead up to the main entrance, that once ever-hospitable open door, now closed and shackled with a rusting chain and padlock. The garden is rampant. As furtive as a pheasant in a fox-infested wood, a single peacock still lives within it, the last of a long line imported when the Contessa's family were ambassadors to the court of Byzantium.

Evening is falling, the sundial shadow of the Campanile has crept across the square and now is a great smudge on the pink walls of the Doges' Palace. The migrating swallows swoop down and settle for the night, roosting in lines on the telephone wires that criss-cross the canals. They are doomed. It is September; they are too late. Only those who flew to Africa by the end of August had any chance of surviving the strenuous journey. From behind the wall, in the dead Contessa's garden, the last of her peacocks cries 'Help! Help!' as it settles down for the long night. And it is time for us to go too, a couple of dodos whose world has become extinct.

'Speak for yourself!' Dominie has just said, reading this over my shoulder.

Bubo Zeylonensis
and
Rollulus Roulroul

7889, Grimaldi Square, Monaco

1960 ~ Portofino.   My father, who no doubt was a male chauvinist pig, said that every man should do at least three things in his life: have a son, plant a tree and write a book. Bubo and Rollulus had done none of those, and had no intention of doing so, and although they called themselves 'importers and exporters' they obviously were crooks, so I was rather surprised that they were friends of his. But he had a lot of strange friends, thanks to the war.

Bubo and Rollulus had been minor pimps in the enormous chain of brothels owned by my great-uncle Henry. Great-uncle Henry did not know he owned these brothels: he thought he was a perfectly ordinary Essex squire with a sideline in textiles (he was a director in Courtaulds Ltd) and a hobby of covering north Essex with bogus Tudor cottages.

The brothels were one of the more successful schemes of SOE during the war. Most of them were along the North African coast, but after Montgomery's successes they spread into Cairo, the Levant, Greece and Italy. The whores used to slip potions into the drinks of their German clients: tank commanders, Luftwaffe pilots and so on, and the effects ranged from instant death, to creeping paralysis, mania or deep pessimism, depending on the recipe (all devised by SOE's boffin, Professor Sir Alexander Todd).

An inconvenient side-effect was that these well-organised brothels started to make money – lots of it, and the bureaucrats in Whitehall got in a frightful tizz and wanted to put the whole thing on a legal and businesslike footing with Profits and Loss balance sheets, payslips and pensions for the employees, office outings and medical checks and inventories on typewriter ribbons and paper clips.

So, to effect this bureaucratic need, my father decided that it all should be officially owned by a nice, vague old thing who would not know what was happening.

'Uncle Henry,' he said one day, 'would you sign this bit of paper? It is a requisition order for some new silk yarn for the Halstead weaving shed.' So the old buffer signed it and made himself the world's biggest pimp: the Pimp of all Pimps, Le Pimp Extraordinaire.

Of course, when the war ended, both the British government and

Courtaulds Ltd were too wet to take any advantage of all this, and the organisation was rapidly taken over by Bubo and Rollulus.

They seemed to me to merely be a couple of ageing playboys whose gin palace had floated into the little harbour of Portofino, where we were holidaying. Rollulus was sleek and dressed entirely in black, with many gold things hanging from wrist and neck; Bubo was very dapper – his suits were tailored in Savile Row, his ties woven in Lyons, his shoes cobbled in Rome and his handkerchiefs embroidered in Venice. His fingernails were of the palest pink, with a slight satin sheen, like pearls; not a whisker sprouted from ear or nostril.

Being extremely rich, and because they now lived in Italy, they had become 'respectable' and 'accepted'. They had a cocktail party aboard the gin palace for some of the local bigwigs, all I really remember of the conversation was something I overheard Rollulus saying to my father: 'I love *all* duchesses, but I love *rich* duchesses best.'

> Colonel Klaus Sapsucker
>
> NATO
>
> Brussels

1998 ~ Brussels.   The warriors of old were muscular great chaps who could bash your helmeted head in with one wallop of their maces, now they are often weedy little brainboxes like Klaus Sapsucker. No Rambo, this American officer; in spite of the rows of medal ribbons which cover the left half of his torso he has never seen any action in the field – but, from his office, he has been able to supervise the 'physical disposal' of a satisfactory number of the enemy. With spectacles, a long, thin, white neck with its hair cut so short and so high it seems almost skinned, he has a questing, anxious voice exactly like Kermit the Frog's.

He has taken me to lunch in the sprawling collection of 'spiders': the office blocks which make up the NATO HQ in Brussels. The place used to be a hive of activity, now it seems inert, like a bumble bees' nest when the queen has died; it feels subdued, with just a few idle drones, hanging about, seemingly aimless, nevertheless, like Sapsucker, full of passion to rectify the insubordination of alien communities.

I feel uneasy, 'For Satan finds some mischief still,
For idle hands to do.'

1999 January ~ AUSTRIA, Vienna

I had a 'special' quick journey from Vienna to Budapest: with only a couple of hours spare, I paid a brief visit to the Ethnographical Museum. This is a neo-Renaissance palace with an astonishing central hall of every sort of marble you can think of, in every form and function: barley-sugar spirals, columns and blocks, stairs and banisters, flooring and walling, statuary and mosaic. There was an interesting exhibit of all the different national dresses of the surprisingly diverse ethnic groups of the former Hungary: twenty-five in all, including Hungarian, Slovakian, Romanian, German, Ruthenian, Croatian and Gypsy. There was another exhibition of clothes: 'from the cradle to the grave'. A bride's trousseau would include all the clothes for her life, including funeral wear. How did they make any allowance for the likelihood of the girl fattening as she aged? The trousseau also formed the total interior equipment for the new household: furniture, linens, crockery, cutlery and cooking kit.

Budapest was foggy and damp; and so it is here, back in Vienna. It is seven o'clock in the evening and I am wandering round the city, waiting for Peter, another Queen's Messenger and former sailor, to arrive from Zagreb; we will then go and dine in the Pink Elephant. There is a public holiday, for it is the Feast of Epiphany, and the streets are almost deserted. The few people about loom silently out of the mist and then fade back into it. It is so quiet I can hear my footsteps echoing off the cobbles and flagging. A stray dog hurries past, its claws clicking on the pavement. The mist swirls around the lamps and condenses and drips off windowsills. Now I hear a melancholy keening: a sobbing, rising and falling. It comes from the doorway of a shop. A man is sitting there. He is swathed in coats and scarves and is hunched over a carpenter's saw which he holds in one hand; there is a fiddle bow in the other. The bow is run over the back of the saw to produce the wailing, the notes change depending on how the saw is being bent or straightened. I put a couple of coins in his hat and drift on, towards St Stephen's.

The spire vanishes into the mist which makes it seem extra tall, as if it was towering up into the clouds like Jack's beanstalk. The cathedral is packed within. The main body of the building is in subdued gloom but, looking over the heads of the praying congregation, I can see the altar lit up by a multitudinous twinkling of candles. Two priests in white and gold are conducting the service. The smoke of incense wafts up to the rib-vaulting high above. I am standing amid a small group of people who probably arrived too late to get a pew. The Lord's Prayer: I do not speak the language, but recognise the intonations. Everyone starts shaking hands with everyone else. I find myself doing it with an old man who has a large carpet bag at his feet. Why should a man in such an immaculate suit and with such brightly polished shoes and sleekly brushed hair be without any teeth? Perhaps, in his haste to come here, he forgot to put them in.

I walk back past the saw player. Two police are standing menacingly over him. Brutes. One is a beefy-looking slob with pale eyes, the other a hard-faced blonde. Typical pip-squeak officials whose instinct is to bully and hector. I don't know the German for 'leave the poor bugger alone, he's doing no harm' so I stop and, having got their attention, give them what I hope is a withering scowl of indignation and contempt.

The blonde policewoman replies with a beaming smile. The sun and moon come out. The whole street lights up. The mist clears. Birds twitter. Flowers bloom. Lambkins and fawns gambol. How wrong I was. She's not hard-faced at all. She is absolutely sweet and charming. Perhaps she is right to move on that smelly tramp.

*   *   *

At the Pink Elephant, I tell Peter I'd been wandering around before he arrived and he asks: 'Glimping or perving?'

'I've never heard of either of those words.'

'They are useful terms we used in the navy. Glimping is looking at girls in a shy, coy way, perving is staring at them brazenly.'

He says it is true that you should not whistle when aboard – in fact on some ships Not Whistling was part of the Standing Orders, but you are allowed to whistle if you are a cook – encouraged even, as it proves you have no food in your mouth.

Schwet V.R. Drongo
Excess Enterprises Ltd
22 Pam-pam Road
Singapore

1993 ~ Singapore. It is lunch time and I am sitting at a pavement restaurant, at the crossroads of Tatam Road and Orchard Road, eating a fried heap of noodles, shrimps, squid, pork and onions. I am using chopsticks to make the meal last longer. As I eat, the people walking past me at the moment are:

a stout woman in short blouse, who sees me staring and looks down to see if a roll of fat is exposed over her belt (it is);

two waddling women carrying shopping bags, both alike – mother and daughter?

a Caucasian in his fifties, wearing jeans and T-shirt, with a small rucksack – huge moustache, hardly any chin and a pony-tail;

a middle-aged businessman, European, nondescript except for an eye-wrenchingly vivid tie and very expensive and well-polished shoes, he . . .

'George!' he shouts.

. . . I don't know him from Adam . . .

'So delightful to see you, what on earth are you doing here?'

. . . *non-English accent – Scandinavian? – Baltic? – probably doesn't know I am a Queen's Messenger otherwise he'd guess why I'm here . . .*

'Good heavens! Fancy seeing *you* here, small world, and all that.'

'Isn't it, though of course you can presume why *I'm* here.'

. . . *haven't a clue. He's a bit furtive now, perhaps he's in the business after all, or maybe one of the military hardware salesmen I used to meet in the Third World when I worked for Courtaulds . . .*

'Oh, yea, of course, heh heh, yea, yup, er, so how's it going?'

'You know: comme ci, comme ça.'

'Of course, yes. The Asian effect. The situation changes, fluctuates, difficult to pin things down, almost impossible to predict.'

'How do you mean?'

. . . *pushed my luck there . . .*

'Well, as you said, comme ci, comme ça.'

'That is so. But, on to other things: how is your family?'

'Thriving, thriving: grandchildren all over the place.'

'Amazing to think of your wife as a grandmother.'

. . . *so he's met Dominie but doesn't know her enough to call her by name . . .*

'And *your* family?'

'Surely you've heard about our little problem?'

'Oh, of course, of course; so still the same then?'

. . . *what on earth am I talking about? . . .*

'Yes. Who told you, incidentally?'

'Oh well, I forget now, but . . . *be bold, try a guess* . . . sad news gets around.'

'Sad!?'

'And good. Sad, or good, news gets around.'

'True, very true.'

. . . *buzz off . . .*

'And Carlos. Poor Carlos.'

'Oh yes, poor old Carlos. How is he?'

'Still dead.'

. . . *oops . . .*

'What I meant was, have they sorted it all out?'

'Yes, but you know how long that sort of thing takes.'

'Yea.'

. . . I do? . . .

He leaves, still babbling obscurities. He has left me his business card. I look at the name. As far as I know, I've never met him in my life.

Cyril H. Dabchick
            (Managing Director)

International Spandrils
                        1556, Frith Street
                        Birmingham

1995 ~ Vienna. Cyril H. Dabchick is a friend of another Queen's Messenger, a gourmet; we wined and dined with him a couple of times in Vienna. He is the sort of man who makes greed a profession and can lead you through a maze of obscure streets to a favourite restaurant where he'll call the owner 'Marcel' and discuss in meticulous detail the marinading of larks' brains or the braising of goats' knuckles. When in such discussion with the patron or head waiter – he would not deign to speak to any lesser menial – he would take off his spectacles and polish them, and think, and purse his lips, and muse again, and put them on, and moisten his lips, and take his specs off again, and repolish them, and muse and nod. By the time he'd decided what to eat I was in a frenzy of frustrated hunger and could have eaten the waiter's boots. He would talk of nothing but food and the places at which he'd eaten it. If you tried to change the subject he would sit in peeved silence, his eyes closed, his fingers drumming the table. Then, when you'd pause, he'd carry on as if you had never said a word.

> Rameses Kagu
>
> El-Gazira Club
>
> Cairo

1975 ~ Cairo. Once, it seemed almost *de rigueur* for a Briton to dislike an Egyptian. I don't know why. Those I have met have struck me as among the most charming of all people: amusing, intelligent and well educated, with a French sophistication, an extrovert exuberance and delight in silly things; they are loyal friends and some of their women are absolutely stunning.

Rameses Kagu was a Coptic Christian. The Copts form about seven per cent of the Egyptian population. Now they are the underdogs of Egyptian society; once they were the aristocracy, rich enough to pay the fines that the Muslim invaders imposed on those who would not convert to Islam. The Copts reckon themselves to be direct heirs of the Pharaohs, hence many of them having names such as Osiris and Isis, Rameses and Amun.

Rameses was my business agent in Cairo: venerable, always immaculately dressed in a pinstriped suit. When I first met him we walked from his office to his club. On the way he bought a red rose for me, which I carried effetely in one hand; my other hand was clasped affectionately in Rameses', and thus I entered the staid precincts of the club to be seen by one of the last people I wanted to meet.

He sidled up to me when I was alone at the bar, Rameses having wandered off.

'I say, Courtauld, a bit weird seeing you coming in like that.'

'Good heavens! Aren't you Bullwanger? The chap at school who was always going around squeezing balls?'

'Tennis balls,' he snapped, looking around for eavesdroppers, 'to strengthen my grip.'

'Did you ever find it useful?'

[149]

'Not much, but I might have, if I'd taken to wandering about hand-in-hand with other fellows.'

Well pleased with his repartee, he departed, sniggering.

1999 February ~ THAILAND

Day 2. My sheep are going to be useful at last. For fifteen years Dominie, Peter, Kerry, dog Jake and I have toiled over those bloody animals: herding, feeding, worming, shearing, paring, dagging, lambing and, as profits have diminished so in proportion has governmental interference increased.

Well, I've sold the lot, and with the money we are going to have a really luxurious holiday in Thailand.

So here we are in Bangkok. Actually Bangkok is just a nickname, the capital's real name is krungthep maha nakorn-amarn rattanakosindra-mahindrayudhya-mahadilokpop noparatana rajdhani mahasathan-amorn piman avatarn satit sakkatultiya vishnukarn prasit, which means The City of Gods, the Great City, the Residence of the Emerald Buddha, the Impregnable City of Ayutthaya of God Indra, the Grand Capital of the World endowed with Nine Precious Gems, the Happy City, abounding in an Enormous Royal Palace which resembles the Heavenly Abode wherein reigns the Reincarnated God, the City given by Indra and built by Vishnukarn.

Dominie and I were met by the travel agent's car and driver who took us from the airport to the hotel through the dust and muggy heat (32° C) of a Bangkok afternoon. Stepping into the luxurious coolness of the Oriental Hotel was like wading into the waters of a mountain tarn. A host of beaming minions swarmed towards us and someone charming and pretty put garlands of orchids and scented jasmine around our shoulders and wrists. From the windows of our corner room we can see a large expanse of the Chao Phraya River to one side, and a view of the city to the other, over the ornately balustraded building which was the original Oriental Hotel. The Oriental is one of the most famous of hotels: for over a decade it was voted 'Best in the World' by international travellers. It is particularly proud of its literary connections, having hosted such guests as Joseph Conrad, Somerset Maugham and Graham Greene.

We liaised with our friends who had already been in Bangkok for two days, and in the evening we all took the hotel ferry to another part of the hotel on the opposite bank to eat at its restaurant called the Terrace Rim Naam. Thai food is noticeably different from the neighbouring Chinese or Indian food: being Buddhist, the Thais do not eat much meat (the butchers are often Chinese); there are many spices, including the ubiquitous lemon grass (a reed, not a fruit) and many sauces, some searingly hot with chillies. (As our guide An-an said to us later: 'We Thais do not get fat, we eat spicy foods and then go to the toilet ALL the time.') Here, in the south, the basic ingredient is rice; in the north it is the noodle. For dinner we started off with river shrimps individually wrapped with sheets of pastry as thin as Bronco loo paper, this was also used to make bags of crabmeat, looking like tiny money bags. We then had 'tom yam kung', a soup of prawns and mushrooms spiced with lemon grass and coriander, followed by 'pla dook', catfish spiced with garlic, ginger, basil and, yet again, lemon grass. While we ate, mist wafted from ice sculptures dotted about to keep us cool; the river craft ceaselessly pottered past us on the Chao Phraya River. This is relatively short (225 miles) but is fed by other rivers from the highlands and plateaux which are on three sides of the great plain in which Bangkok is sited. This plain, one of the richest of the world's rice-growing areas, is as flat as a pancake and full of canals (called khlongs), some of which enter the city – hence the nickname 'The Venice of the East'. The basic design of the Bangkok boat is long and thin and elegant with an extremely high prow which rears out of the water. It is called a 'rua hang yao', which means 'long-tailed boat', the tail being the very long propeller shaft. This counterweights the motor at the other end. The motor is an unnecessarily massive machine, full of pipes and manifolds and exhausts which boom and puke and blow. I think there is probably a lot of kudos in having a huge and noisy engine. Other boats include smart cruisers owned by luxury hotels, sampans rowed by traders, high-eaved passenger boats and ferries, police launches, slender canoes paddled by monks, determined little tugs towing convoys of great black barges of steel, or sometimes their earlier equivalent, rice-barges built from strakes of teak as beautifully crafted as if by a cooper on a beer barrel.

Day 3. While Dominie and I are hanging about in the hotel lobby, waiting for our luggage to be brought down so that our car and driver can take us to the domestic airport, one of the staff comes to talk: his natty white uniform with brass buttons shows that he is a porter. He is middle-aged and dapper, with his hair greased down flat and glossy; he is small, even for a Thai, but typically polite and smiling. A brass plate on his uniform states that his name is Lickit.

He speaks – rather, he orates:

'Let me have men about me that are fat; sleek-headed men such as sleep o'nights.'

I somehow feel that he is being extremely personal and cheeky, in an intellectual way:

'You are the porter?'

'What's in a name? That which we call a rose by any other name would smell as sweet.'

'That's as maybe, but we have been waiting for our luggage for ages. We were told it would be over there, where my wife is waiting.'

> 'There's language in her eye, her cheek, her lip,
> Nay, her foot speaks; her wanton spirits look out
> At every joint and motive of her body.'

More impertinence, nevertheless he and I go to inspect the space behind the concierge's desk. Nothing there but someone else's suitcases. But there is a form on the counter with our room number on it. My peculiar little acquaintance takes it:

'Let us make an honourable retreat, though not with bag and baggage, yet with scrip and scrippage.'

He disappears, and rapidly reappears with a lesser menial pushing a trolley laden with our cases. Our car is loaded; before I enter I turn to thank Peculiar Little Acquaintance. He smiles meaningfully at me and says:

> 'The quality of mercy is not strain'd,
> It droppeth as the gentle rain from heaven
> Upon the place beneath: it is twice bless'd;
> It blesseth him that gives and him that takes.'

I take the hint and press a 50 baht note into his outstretched palm and we drive off with his parting words intoning after us:

> 'Whether we shall meet again, I know not.
> Therefore our everlasting farewell take:
> For ever, and for ever, farewell, Cassius!
> If we do meet again, why, we shall smile!
> If not, why then, this parting was well made.'

In the car Dominie and I read notes he has given us. They are written on the back of the hotel's luggage labels. Dominie's note is simple, and in flowing copper-plate: 'To business that we love we rise betime, And go to't with delight.' This is followed by Shakespeare's name and dates.

My label is covered with minute writing. It begins: 'The Original Mind, a mind in natural condition is "free", "void", "luminous", and "non-suffering" at contact and feeling. A void mind or a selflessness mind (intrinsic mind = neutral state) is the Middle Mind, appearing as the basic mind.' After about three hundred more words in a similarly weird waffle it ends: 'Nibbana – a clean, clear, calm mind! One obtains the highest good of humanity here and now, the actual present reality.'

Hmm. My mind is all of an a-mazement.

As we emerged from the Baggage Collection Hall in Chiang Mai airport another smiling, stocky person bustled towards us: 'You are Mr and Mrs Jenkinson and Mr and Mrs Courtauld. I am your guide for the next eight days. My name is Mel Gibson.'

'Good morning,' I said politely, 'do you prefer to be called Mel or Mr Gibson?'

[153]

His smile wavered a bit. 'That was a joke,' he said.

'What was?'

'The Mel Gibson.'

'What's funny about that?'

'Mel Gibson is actually a famous film star,' Dominie explained, wearily.

'Well, he can't be very famous if I've never heard of him.'

'All his travelling about makes George a bit unworldly,' Dominie explained to the others.

The guide, somewhat crestfallen that his joke had had such a laborious reception, told us that his name is really An-an and that the driver of our mini-bus – also for the next eight days – is named Un. Un looks like An-an but his smile is less professional. At present, he is driving us through the bustle of the city of Chiang Mai. An-an speaks in a staccato gabble. I can understand only about one word in ten but the gist is that Chiang Mai, 'the Rose of the North', is the ancient capital of what is now north Thailand. It was founded in 1292 by a King Mengrai in the fertile valley of the River Ping (I love these names, we have already met Dong, Pong, Klang, Klong, Bang, Bong, Phi-Phi, Moo and Bophit). The old city is a mile-by-mile square bounded by a wall and moat; the former is quite impressive at the corner bastions and the five entrance gates, but elsewhere it is in irregular chunks, like long piles of bricks heaped at random. The city has spread outside the moat into a mixture of wats (temple-monasteries), office blocks, new hotels and rows of old housing, all bound together by a plethora of overhead cables. There are many areas set aside for the manufacturing of local industries and handicrafts such as lacquered and enamelled boxes, wood carvings, silver jewellery, painted umbrellas. 'I take you to many, I find you very good prices,' says An-an.

'Thank you, but as far as I am concerned you need not bother,' I say, 'I loathe shopping.'

'The customer is always right,' says An-an glumly.

Now, in the half-hour drive between the city and our hotel we can see the rapid development of farmland and old housing into the buildings of modern life: a hodge-podge of orchards and market gardening and ribbon development. Here is a timber yard; a new bungalow has been built in the garden of a wooden shack, the entrance to a barracks (smartly signed 'Pack Squadron'), its pastures to either side are full of mules, a mango orchard, more old wooden shacks, ribbon development of shops with balconied flats above them, garages, municipal buildings and offices, another garage, next to it a car showroom – not many cars, mostly open-backed trucks (also the dominant vehicle on the roads), some allotments with restaurants or vegetable shops adjacent, selling their produce, bougainvillaea wreathing expensive garden railings, a banana plantation, a palm grove, more shops . . .

'That is a free hotel,' says An-an, pointing to a large building covered with flags and draped with bunting: another of his jokes – it is a borstal, celebrating the opening of a new extension.

Outside many buildings there are shrines (An-an calls them 'spirit houses'). They are about the size of a large bird-table and carry an image of Buddha – or sometimes a Hindu god – sitting in a pointed-roofed pavilion. The flat platform on which this erection is placed is heaped with food and bowls of water and vases full of smouldering joss sticks; festooned about are garlands of flowers and maybe, at ground level, there are potted plants. An-an explains that they are lures to attract away both good and bad spirits from the nearby buildings, both spirits can be a nuisance when indoors. Sometimes, when we pass one, Un takes both hands off the wheel and, bowing, presses his palms together in front of his face in the traditional Thai greeting. The mini-bus meanders about at liberty as he does this.

We see many domestic fowl. At first I thought that they were birds of prey, kites or such-like: dark, mean-looking creatures with close-fitting plumage and long legs in black tights and scaly thigh boots, viciously spurred. Cock fighting is still a local sport. Also, oddly enough, is fish fighting, An-an says.

Outside the entrance of most domestic housing there is a type of large black cauldron on a stand; they look rather like the pots cannibals are meant to cook missionaries in. An-an tells me that they are not of iron, but of rubber, and they are 'what you call dustbins.'

We turn into a drive edged with formal plantings and arrive at the Regent Resort. Our 'pavilion suite' is a free-standing teak-built building, most of which is taken up by a large bedroom. Leading from it, over a balustraded walkway, is our veranda or 'sala', surrounded by trees and large-leaved plants. Our bathroom is the *pièce de resistance*. It is a large glass case abutted to the rear wall. An enclosing wall has been built around the case so no one can look in. Tropical plants and flowers are growing between glass and wall. At night, when having a bath, one can turn lights on which illuminate this vegetation so one has the impression of bathing in the middle of a jungle.

Having unpacked, we wander through the tropical gardens to have drinks and then lunch on a terrace overlooking a dell. In the nearest part of this dell there are pools, with red and blue flowering lotuses spangling the water's surface; they are edged with clumps of sedge and reed; further off are small paddy fields, the rice ready to be harvested; at the far end is a thatched hut on stilts, under it laze the hotel's water buffalo – Mr Clay, Mrs Mud and baby Nin. In the far background we can just see the outline of a range of mountains, half hidden in a scented haze which is smoke from burning forests, set alight by the Hill Tribesmen practising their slash-and-burn method of agriculture.

Most of the clientèle here are the rich and rare. The Jenkinsons overheard four old mid-European ladies talking about the servant problems in Vienna before the war.

Day 4. A day of wat watching in Chiang Mai. A wat has a variety of uses: it serves as a temple, with living quarters for the monks who tend it; often there may be an associated school, usually the only school if in a village, where it also may serve as the village hall – the meeting place for the local council and for community activities. There may also be a shrine containing an important relic, and graves of local worthies. A wat is usually in a walled or fenced compound: there is an ornate central hall, called a 'bot', and outbuildings which may range from a stark dormitory block for novice monks to shrines and pagodas. Usually, there is not much that is old, except for the site, because paying for renovation or complete reconstruction is considered a pious action. But some of the images that we saw were of great antiquity, in Wat Chiang Man we saw a crystal Buddha 1800 years old and a tiny marble plaque aged 2500. An-an led us from wat to wat until we were in a daze, our minds a jumbled confusion of soaring roofs and dragon-tipped gables, staircases with seven-headed snakes acting as banister rails, a profusion of twinkling and glittering mosaic in mirror and coloured chips of ceramic, steepled spires and steps and the smell of incense, the murky recesses in the far ends of bots where a host of images gazed at us in impassive scrutiny, and everywhere the gleam of gold. Other impressions included the women selling caged birds. An-an said: 'Buy one, I get you good price, then release it and when it flies away it takes your bad lucks with it.' Some images of Buddha were covered with little rectangles of gold leaf. An-an told us: 'You glue on the gold where you want to be cured, or on a part of the body which is important to you. A footballer will put a bit on Buddha's foot, I put a bit on his mouth, because I rely on talking for my business.' In some wats we noticed fan-like blades on the end of broomsticks. An-an explained: 'They are not fans. They are screens. A young monk will carry one beside a more senior monk, and if he thinks that this senior monk will catch sight of some lady's underwear or other forbidden things he will put the screen in front of this senior monk's eyes.' I pointed out that many of the idols showed Buddha with a huge nose. 'That is because Buddha came from India, and the Indians, like you Europeans, have very very fine and good and not at all laughable big noses.' Before entering any wat we had to take our shoes off: on the entrance steps my size ten-and-a-halves looked like barges at anchor amid flotillas of dainty little raft-like sandals and canoe-shaped slippers. I think Dominie has taken rather a dislike to wats. The last straw was a round board upon which was written:

The circle of life
with the old, illness and
after that gets died, so what's
going on the circle
~~
?

Really jolly,' said Dominie.

Buddhism has its attractions. Some of its followers are gentle and stoic and well mannered, and some of its fables and parables are full of common sense and kindness and even wit. However, it can engender sloth, and an impassive resignation to and acceptance of fate. Alternatively, the idea of reincarnation can keep one on one's toes: better be good, unless one wants to be reborn as a flea in a beggar's underpants.

Now we are back on the hotel terrace, having dinner. The sun has set over the mountains opposite, moonlight is reflected in the waters of the paddy fields. Among them, a man is lighting flares, the paraffin torch he is using swings in arcs as he walks from flare to flare. A drum quietly thumps and a stick zither tinkles, frogs start to chirr in a clump of reed just below. From a distant pavilion a paper balloon rises, trailing a stream of sparks, then another, and another; the little balloons, kept aloft by tiny lanterns inside them, float high and far until hidden by the palms on the hillside to leeward. (An-an later told us that they are carrying away annoying spirits, so it is very bad luck if one of the balloons lands in your garden.)

We walk back to our pavilion: past the ornamental pools where the flowers of frangipani have been placed to float above the drifting of the Koi carp, past clumps of lush-leaved plants, past the swimming pool, where torch-flames reflect in the waters, past a terracotta statue of a pig. On its explicatively crafted fundament someone has glued a sliver of gold leaf.

Day 8. An-an has told us that there are about two thousand wild elephants left in the country and three thousand domesticated ones. We are about to ride on one of the latter.

The elephants are corralled at their 'station' beside the Pai Hai River. One of them is rather small. To my chagrin – and Dominie's relief – this is at the head of the line and the one we must mount. Her name is Boonjune, the mahout is Toonong. He has the physical properties of a spider monkey, which is just as well: Boonjune is so small that now Dominie and I are aboard there is no room for Toonong on the elephant's neck; he has to perch on the top of her head like a peculiar hat. The howdah is merely a pew for two; Dominie had a frightful job boarding it (she's bad enough getting on to a horse), and now we are seated we stick out to either side as if we are on the outer wings of a ship's bridge. Toonong scratches a signal with his toes behind Boonjune's ears and we move off, following two other larger elephants, one crammed with a German family, the other with a couple of French homosexuals from our hotel, both with shaven heads and earrings, one stripped to the waist to disclose a back as hairy as a gorilla's. I grumble that they are all pleased that our elephant is much smaller than theirs. Dominie tells me not to be so competitive. Boonjune waddles down a steep bank, wades through the river, and then follows the other elephants who sashay along a track worn in the bush. Dominie notices that they put their rear feet in the prints of their front ones, which gives them their swinging motion; as each foot is put down it puffs out like a marshmallow.

We enter the forest. It is silent, no birdsong, no sough of the wind through trees: it is so quiet that we can hear the occasional brittle 'click' as an autumn-dead leaf of a teak tree falls on to the forest bed. The elephants drift between the tree-trunks like grey ghosts. Thais believe that every person has a spirit companion, a sort of *Doppelgänger* called a *chetabhut*. It leaves its human companion during dreams or times of care. If a man is walking alone in a forest and hears footsteps behind him and looks back and sees nobody, he has heard his *chetabhut*. But I cannot hear any ghostly footsteps.

Toonong scrabbles behind Boonjune's ears to manoeuvre her into a thicket. Dominie and I are surrounded by leaves and tendrils. Grapefruit-sized melon-like fruits are hanging from a creeper. Toonong unsheathes the machete which he carries in a scabbard on his back and bashes away at the herbage, managing, eventually, to cut off three of the fruit which release clouds of grey powder from their surface. Some red tree ants fall off a branch and land on my leg; one or two bite, one or two scurry about to find anywhere interesting to nest.

'Ouch! Hoi! Let's get out of here!' I complain to Toonong. He prods about with his toes but Boonjune is either too young or too bolshie to understand; she remains rooted to the spot. Ants trickle down. They quest around. Dominie gets the giggles and then cramp and proceeds to writhe and gasp. Toonong taps on Boonjune's trunk and she reaches up with it and collects one of the fruits; it disappears into her mouth and there is a loud pop and crunch. The elephant then condescends to back out of the thicket and we wade up a small stream, having lost contact with the others.

We are back at the elephant station. I feed Boonjune her tip: a bunch of bananas. They cost about tuppence a banana. Dominie apologises to Boonjune for the three missing ones, which I have eaten.

*   *   *

The river craft are laid on a shingle bank below the elephant station. They are similar to the long-tailed boats of Bangkok: about forty-five feet long and four feet wide at the most, a high uprearing stem, a powerful engine at the stern, with the propeller at the end of a long shaft. There is a crew of two: the driver by the engine, and a lookout perched at the top of the bows. Both are small and wrinkled and dusky, like Toonong. When we get amidships and lounge with our backs to the gunwale, our heads are only a couple of feet above water level.

Off we go, the powerful engine sending us skimming over the surface of the river. The river banks are lush, with clumps of rush and reed, occasionally a banana grove; further off the ground rears up into cliffs. The water is rough and choppy in the shallows, smooth in the deeps; boulders rear out of the water here and there. We see an elephant standing in the water, ignoring us.

'WELCOME TO LONG NECK VILLAGE (Padong)' says a notice on the river bank. We disembark on the shingly beach. Children paddle in the waters beside us; the village is above us, further up the hill.

There are eight thousand Padongs in Thailand. There are more in Burma, the country of their origin. The rings that their women wear round their necks, arms and legs are in imitation of their ancestor, a dragon, some of them say; others say it is a protection from tigers. The rings are put round the little girls' necks when they are aged about four; four or five rings to start with – a ring is added every three years. The most rings worn were twenty-five; they eventually weigh about four kilos. They stretch the neck about nine inches and deform the neck vertebrae and bend down the collar bones and upper ribs. Another four kilos' weight of brass rings are worn round the arms and legs. If a woman displeases her husband he can take the rings off and her neck snaps, or she suffocates.

We walk up the path of beaten earth which is the high street. The houses of the village are cosy: they are low, with verandas; under their thatched roofs, the walls are woven from strips of bamboo in a twill or hopsack-type weave. There are stacks of logs beside or under the dwellings. Chickens peck about; dogs laze. I see my first Padong. I had thought she may be elegant, like a swan. She is grotesque, like an ostrich: her tiny little head is balanced atop the tall brass column; she has a cautious, uneasy gait, as if fearful that her golfball head may roll off its tee.

An-an introduces us to an old crone. She is sitting bolt upright – no option – on a step of her veranda. She has a prim, rather smug face, with a fringe of still-dark curls; she is chewing betel nuts, which makes her look even more fearsome as they stain her lips into a great red splodge. Her head-dress is a piece of cloth which hangs down her back and her clothes are mostly yellow and blue. She smiles at us and natters. An-an translates: 'She is called Apungsa and is seventy years old; she wants you to sit next to her so that I can photograph you with your camera. Then she will sell you a photo of herself very cheap.' Torn between embarrassment and wanting not to hurt her feelings we sit; we are photographed; we buy.

Most of the population in the centre of the village seem to be sitting on their verandas, an array of 'ethnic art' laid out before them: embroidered bags and purses, lengths of cloth, dolls, brass bangles. One of the women is suckling an infant.

'What a sweet baby!' exclaims Dominie.

The word 'baby' amuses the mother and she smilingly repeats it. She is quite pretty. But think of having a mother like that at school. I found it hard enough to explain away a mother who was French and who wore hats covered with masses of feathers. How would one explain away a mother with a nine-inch neck and a stone's weight of brass rings clanking about?

A flock of tourists wanders past. They are gawping in astonishment at the ringed women. The ringed women are equally astonished: that man with hair all over his mouth and chin! that other man with no hair at all on the top of his head! (mange?); that woman in short trousers! (her thighs! so white! so fat! the sticking-out veins squiggling all over them!); that other woman who has painted her lips and fingernails red and dyed her hair yellow! these people's eyes (with lids, and blue! like a pig's); those children with pieces of metal all over their front teeth! And why are they pointing and laughing? Are they not being taught any manners? The long-necked women are not ill-mannered, they do not stare back; they just peek out of the corner of their eyes.

Day 9. To get to Mae Hong Son we had driven north and then west; to return to Chiang Mai we will do the other two sides of a rectangle by driving south and then east: An-an said it will be about 350 kilometres and take ten hours.

On the way we have diverted to a Meo village: a half-hour drive uphill along a small, winding lane. In all, there are about a hundred thousand Meos (also called Hmangs). Two hundred years ago they fled from China during a civil war. Un parks on a patch of beaten earth near the centre of the village. We are above much of it, we can look down little vales at the houses strewn below: people sit in colourfully dressed groups under the shade of trees; other bright patches of colour are encapsulated in the washing draped over fencing. Further off we can see banana groves and fields in which, judging by the stacks heaped up near the houses, they have been growing maize, pumpkins and cabbages; there are also heaps of firewood by the dwellings. The houses are built on the ground, not on stilts. We wander down, rather embarrassed; the people stare at us and, although not disagreeable, do not look welcoming. They are very small. The basic clothing seems to be black, with colourful panels or strips of embroidery: black trousers, a dark skirt banded with intricate embroidery, sometimes a huge black hat like a balloon. We pass a woman winnowing with a round-headed fan; she shuffles the heap of rice with her bare feet as she fans. We are led by An-an to a group of women sitting in a doorway. They are embroidering, using the same cross-stitch that Dominie has been using on the tapestry she has been lugging all over Thailand. We buy a couple of embroidered purses, smile lamely and sidle off. There is a long-snouted black pig in a cheerless sty with no food or water. Like the houses, the pen is built of bamboo, a material which can be used in every way: split and hammered flat as walling, half-round as ventilation bars, in the round as roof rafters, split longways as guttering.

'It does not last long, twelve years perhaps,' says An-an.

'Same age as my hat,' I say.

An-an stares at my hat – made of woven straw in Portugal. 'It is an antique!' he exclaims. 'Why have termites not eaten it?'

Another diversion to another hill village, this one of White Karens (there are also Red Karens, the difference being their complexions). An-an and I leave Un dozing and Dominie embroidering ('I refuse to stare at any more people'). We walk down a narrow path of beaten earth. There is a smell of autumn; dry leaves rustle and crunch underfoot; then there is an unidentifiable regular thumping. We enter the village. It is in sad ruin: many houses seem to be abandoned and are moulting thatch and are broken-backed and sinking back into the soil, tilting and deflating like dying elephants. The thumping turns out to be a rice-mill-cum-dehusker: a woman stamps at one end of a see-sawing beam; a wooden hammer at the other thumps rice into a bowl. Chickens peck the spillage around it, but the woman seems too lethargic to call them off. Two other women lounge and stare from under another house (these ones are on stilts). There are no other people around. Three dreadfully thin piglets wander past. All seems despair and degeneration, without purpose or future.

Day 16. Having spent five more days being idle in a luxury villa on the island of Phuket (whose 'P', disappointingly, is pronounced not as in Phoebe, but as in Peter), we land at Heathrow at 05.15 and are met by Henrietta who very kindly has driven a hundred miles to pick us up.

As she drives us round the M25, up the M11 and along the A120 flocks of rooks wheel over the plough lands, pheasants lurk in the furrows, pigeons flit from wood to wood, gulls are flying inland, blackbirds and starlings fidget in the hedges, a skein of geese flies overhead: within ten minutes of dawn I see more birds than I did in a whole fortnight in Thailand.

We are *home*! Snowdrops are blooming in drifts in the garden.

The sheep pastures are silent.

KURT LAMMERGEYER

Senior Sales Representative

Scandan Household Textile Corp

Malmö

Sweden

1991 ~ London to Rio de Janeiro flight. I have forgotten what Kurt Lammergeyer looked like except that he had rather glittery spectacles and very pale eyes. He was a neighbour on the aeroplane and told me that he was delighted to be going to Rio de Janeiro because there, like Ankara and New York, he could sit in the streets having his shoes polished; sometimes he had them polished four or five times a day, between business appointments (his customers were mostly hotel groups). He said that in the United States he could buy sandwiches and eat them while being buffed, but the sandwiches in Turkey were non-existent so, there, he sometimes had to decide whether to have his shoes cleaned instead of having lunch. He liked looking at the tops of people's heads, he said, not only at that of the person polishing, but also, from the elevated position of some of the seats, at the tops of the heads of passers-by. 'Did it give you a feeling of power?' I asked. No, he said, looking down at a person's head, especially if a menial, made him feel very benign. He loved the double-decker buses in London, but was very disappointed in the quality and quantity of its boot boys.

'The one in Burlington Arcade is very good, however.'

Colonel Steven Corncrake
Defence Attaché
The British Embassy
Mexico City

1997 ~ Mexico City. Our Defence Attaché in Mexico is a very big man, a better diplomat than most professional diplomats; he was formerly a cavalryman, but he had also served in the Trucal and Oman Scouts. We had dinner together in Mexico City, with some television people who were on return from a South American fracas. We ate huitlacoche, which is a cob of maize covered with a rare mould. It occurs naturally and is not possible to procreate so, like truffles, it is a great delicacy. Its consistency is a bit like cheese, and it tastes slightly cheesy-cum-mushroomy. Then I had a huge helping of gristly lumps set alongside a heap of brown mush (mashed beans), all artfully surrounded by a tough-leafed vegetable. One television man said that the pollution problems of Mexico City are partly caused by the enormous amount of beans the people eat, also peppers and chillies.

Steven said that when he retired from Arabia a feast was given in his honour: dead goat, its head lolling about in the gravy. The host thumbed out an eyeball and gave it to him; he, not wanting to hurt feelings, ate it, but in one gulp – no chewing and munching. After a while he felt a bit of string between his teeth. Pulled at it – the whole eyeball came up.

This reminded someone else who told us that he had a friend who spent many months doing an anthropological study on a tribe of natives in the middle of the Amazonian jungle. When he departed, they had a feast in his honour. At the start of the meal he had to drink a bowl full of dark liquor. Mentally holding his nose he drained it. He saw a monkey's head at the bottom: well boiled, as soft as a suet dumpling. Thought, 'Oh God, I suppose I must . . .' Ate it: brains, bones, eyes – the lot.

The headman turned to him and said: 'My *Goodness*, you English are *disgusting*. You'll do *anything* to be liked.'

Old Joke:

FIRST CANNIBAL: Gracious, this missionary is tough.
SECOND CANNIBAL: Maybe, but he's better than the chops we
    used to get at the London School of Economics.

WILFRED RONALD
POCHARD
Sloughbottom Farm Seeds
Steeple Bumpstead
Essex

1995 ~ Ulaan Baatar.   I met Wilfred Ronald Pochard in the Steppe Inn, our packing-case-cum-club house in Ulaan Baatar. He was trying to sell Brussels sprouts and cabbage seeds to the Mongolians. He had a very red face, and the extraordinary tufts of hair in each ear hole were like hedgehogs, or sea urchins, completely round and prickly. He wore an anti-freezing garb patented by himself: something between a track suit and a pair of pyjamas in ginger-coloured camelhair. I have once seen a man dressed up as a gorilla for a 'Kissagram'; should the Kissagram people have wanted an orang-utan, Wilf Pochard would have sufficed. It would have been a kindness thus to employ him, no-one seems to have told him that the Mongolians call people who eat vegetables 'weed-eaters'.

He's dead now — tractor accident.

1999 March ~ JORDAN, The Trans-Jordan Desert

The streets of Amman are almost deserted as I set off in my hired car at 8.30 on a cool but sunny morning, for it is Eid ul-Fitr, a Muslim celebration rather like our Easter. After the Lent-like abstentions of Ramadan, Eid is a three-day holiday, starting, by the looks of it, with a good lie-in, and continuing with a feast of specially fattened sheep.

I have seen a couple of the sheep being led up the streets, all primped and washed and fluffed up, smug and pleased with themselves, unaware of their imminent doom; now that I have emerged into the countryside I am seeing goats, the only animals able to browse on rubble and empty plastic water-bottles.

I am driving along the ancient Kings' Highway, the 5000-year-old road which starts at the ancient Red Sea port of Aqaba and goes north through what is now Jordan and Syria into Turkey. It is the road of Iron Age traders, of the warring tribes of the Old Testament; the Hittites marched down it to invade Egypt; the Egyptians marched up it to destroy the army of Nebuchadnezzar – then fled back down it; traders from Phoenicia and India paid their tolls to the Nabataeans of Petra, whose city-state ruled part of the land it traversed. Its surface was worn by sandals, shoes and boots of Persians, Greeks, Romans, Byzantines, Crusaders, the pilgrims to Christendom or to Mecca – and now by the flip-flops, trainers or brogues of tourists.

After the first twenty-five miles I arrive at the market town of Madaba. It is bustling and scruffy; people wander in the middle of the road, stall-holders and shopkeepers are laying out their wares – all food, presumably for the normal last-minute panic buying from whoever is cooking today's feasts.

Madaba has a long history, first being mentioned in Numbers, chapter XXI. After its periods as Moabite, Hellenic and Nabataean settlements it became an important Roman centre, then a Byzantine bishopric. It withered into disuse and crumbled into decay to be revived as 'The City of Mosaics': famed for its richness in the mosaics which were the flooring – and sometimes walling – of its Byzantine churches and villas.

The tesserae from which these mosaics are made are small blocks about a centimetre square. They are made from local stone whose colours are surprisingly varied: red, blue, green, terracotta, beige, yellow, black and white and many variations in between. The craftsmen worked from pattern books which circulated throughout the Byzantine civilisation, but many local specialities of design or subject were included. The best-known mosaic is the 'Madaba Map'. Made in AD 560 as the flooring of a sixth-century church, it charts the Holy Land from Jordan and Palestine in the north to Egypt in the south. It is a picture map: cities are depicted with their main buildings in place; some rivers have pulley-driven ferries which indicate fordable places; there are fish in the rivers; elsewhere are animals and trees, according to their preferred habitat, so that they indicate desert, oasis, mountainous regions, scrubland or swamp. The map was about twenty feet wide by fifty feet long and made from over two and a quarter million tesserae. It was almost entire until the Greek patriarch in Jerusalem commissioned an architect to build a new church over it, in 1896. The design and ensuing construction destroyed sections of the map, as the architect thought it of no importance. He is now on my list of people of minor but significant detestability, which includes William Dowsing the

[167]

Window Smasher, John Knox the Woman Hater, Henry VIII and Baron Beeching of British Rail.

There are many other beautiful mosaics in the local basilicas and churches and private houses. Having seen the milling crowds which are increasing every moment, I have decided not to see any of them today. I will carry on another six miles to Mount Nebo instead. Of all religious sites in Jordan, the most important to the 'three religions of the Book' (Judaism, Christianity and Islam) is this mountain. It is mentioned several times in the Bible, the most memorable incident being in Deuteronomy, chapter XXXIV, verses 1–4:

> And Moses went up from the plains of Moab unto the mountain of Nebo, to the top of Pisgah, that is over against Jericho. And the Lord shewed him all the land of Gilead, unto Dan,
> And all Naphtali, and the land of Ephraim, and Manasseh, and all the land of Judah, unto the utmost sea,
> And the south, and the plain of the valley of Jericho, the city of palm trees, unto Zoar.
> And the Lord said unto him, This is the land which I sware unto Abraham, unto Isaac, and unto Jacob, saying, I will give it unto thy seed: I have caused thee to see it with thine eyes, but thou shalt not go over thither.

There should be a good view from there, if nothing else.

It is first recorded as a Christian site by Aetheria, one of those rich, devout and rather dotty early Christian women who went hunting for Holy Places. They generally went to the west of the River Jordan (now Israel/Palestine) for the New Testament, and to the east (now Jordan) for the Old Testament. Aetheria trekked here in AD 394 and found a small church containing the tomb of Moses (one of several, as 'no man knoweth of his sepulchre' – Deuteronomy).

The buildings on the site flourished and expanded, but by the mid-sixteenth century had become abandoned and ruined. Franciscan monks started excavations and reconstructions in 1933, and I have a copy of their guide book. The Introduction was charmingly written by one of the early archaeologists, Father Bellarmino Bagatti. His fellow archaeologists included Brother Jerome Mihaic, an ex-gaucho and hunter, and founder and driving force of the excavations; Father Sylvester Saller, 'tall and massive in the brown habit . . . went to work with his head well wrapped in the keffieh leaving just his eyes and nose visible. The sun, however, always burnt the point of his nose'; Brother Baramila, who, 'although he did not have a welcoming aspect was followed [by the locals] because he hunted objects by the walls and went to the mountain with his small instruments, the altimeter and compass, to mark who knows what.' Their site guardian was Hajj Saleh el-Wukhyan, who, 'faithful to his religion extended his mat easily on the ground to make genuflections and bows at the fixed hours of prayer. With a rifle slung on his back and cartridges at his side, he liked to be photographed by the tourists and pilgrims . . . He could not understand money being thrown away on excavations instead of using it to buy wives.'

The monks excavated a typical Byzantine basilica. The original seen by Aetheria had been ruined by earthquakes; the basilica unearthed was the replacement constructed in AD 597. Now, the buildings on site include the old church, restored and reroofed, and an adjacent monastery of the Franciscans of Terrasanta. From outside, the basilica is low and unimpressive. I walk round it. Excavations have laid bare neat rectangles and squares of limestone walling, the remains of living and communal quarters, and accessories such as ovens, granaries and tombs; a line of pigsty-sized cells was possibly for the resident hermits. At the far west I look over the wall of the garden-like atrium to see exactly the same view that Moses and God talked about: the land tumbles in hillocks and hummocks down to the floor of the Jordan Valley, two and a half thousand feet below; the waters of the Dead Sea have a steely tinge; some green tufts mark the oasis of Jericho; the mountains of Judaea loom as shadowy shapes beyond the western shore; and further on, in the far horizon, blurred by a sand storm, there is the faint outline of the Mount of Olives – 'The Land of Milk and Honey'. It all looks pretty bleak and barren to me.

And the Lord said unto Moses, Make thee a fiery serpent, and set it up upon a pole: and it shall come to pass, that everyone that is bitten, when he looketh upon it, shall live.

And Moses made a serpent of brass, and put it upon a pole (Numbers, chapter XI, verses 8–9).

To my right there is an excellent bit of modern art, a metal-wrought representation of Moses' standard. By Giovanni Fantoni, stark and simple, it is in the shape of an ankh; the serpent twines up the pole and loops over the top, the cross-bars have been cleverly styled in the beautiful flattened-out curves of the horns of a wild goat. (I wonder if the artist knows that.)

Immediately below me are the flat roofs of the Franciscan monastery: they lie there in utter silence, slightly sinister. What is happening there, inside?

Inside the basilica there is a wide central nave lined with eight pillars per side; to the other side of these are the aisles, baptistery and side chapels. The chancel and rounded nave have been adapted from the original trefoil-shaped church. They are to the east. (Now, why is that? I was always told that all altars in England face east because that is where Jerusalem is, but Jerusalem is due west from here.)

The great glory of this church lies in its mosaics. They are displayed either flat on the ground (these are the originals, *in situ*) or reinforced and hung upright (these have been brought in from excavations elsewhere). The first impression is of the gentle subtlety of their colours; the second is how much they look like carpets, particularly the ones with simple designs based on squares, lozenges, quatrefoils or flowers. The most interesting mosaic is a large one depicting scenes of hunting and livestock raising, including two horsemen with hounds, killing a boar and a bear; a herdsman protecting a zebu from a lion; a shepherd sitting on a rock under a tree and watching his little browsing flock of sheep and goats; a boy leading a camel and a zebra, both harnessed; and a negro holding an ostrich by a leash.

In the apse, above the altar, there are three windows by Salvatore Cavallini. Of vividly coloured stained glass, they depict events in the life of Moses. They also illustrate how in comparison to the unrefined, naive, faded remnants of Antiquity, modern art, backed by the latest techniques and with the added skills of two millennia, can be in utterly shocking bad taste: tawdry, garish and vulgarly intrusive; at the far end of the church the eye-wrenching, greedy colours overwhelm the gentle honey and cream and chocolate tinges which percolate throughout the remainder of the church; the 'cardboard cut-out' shapes are crude caricatures compared with the ethereal, dream-eyed figures of Rome and Byzantium.

Twenty-five miles later, I reach a massive crack in the ground, two and a half miles wide and 1600 feet deep, cleft open by an earthquake and then gouged out further by a river. The road writhes and meanders in hairpin bends down its precipitous sides for about eight miles, then another nine miles up. It is the Wadi Mujib: 'the Grand Canyon of Jordania'. The River Arnon which flows along it was the old boundary between the Moabites to the south and the Amorites to the north. The high terraced and stratified cliffs and slopes look desolate and barren, but plants grow here, some rare, and there are Syrian wolves, foxes and mongooses, snakes and lizards.

The Holy Land has hundreds of Crusader castles and forts. Their principal uses were as residences for the local rulers and their families, as centres of local government and economic supervision, and as barracks. When the Crusaders themselves became increasingly defensive, so their castle fortifications became stronger and more ingenious. However, the main strategic theory of the Crusaders was always 'attack is the best method of defence', and it was the ability to billet fighting soldiers that became the most important use of a castle. Before the Crusades, for example in Norman England, the basic design of a castle was a keep, which acted as main residence and final defensive post; the surrounding protection was a wall, sometimes augmented with a moat, or with cliffs, or with revetments reinforcing an earthen mound. The Crusades revolutionised the European theory of castellation, partly because of the prototypes of local Byzantine fortresses, partly because of the persistence and numerical superiority of the enemy. The new principle was that there should be areas of mutual protection within the fortress: that rings and pockets of defence should overlook one another, and walls should be flanked by projecting towers.

Kerak is a good example of this. 'Crusader in origin, Arab in repair, modern in decay, still a thing of beauty,' says my guide book. Actually, it is not Crusader in origin; the site was too good for others to ignore and over one thousand years before the Crusades it was a Moabite stronghold – cursed several times by the prophet Isaiah. Later, it was depicted in the Madaba Map, as a Christian walled city. The castle was built in 1136–42 by 'Lord Payen the Butler', who made it his headquarters. Later Crusader lords added towers and a dry moat which cut into the neck of land leading to the main massif on which the castle was built. The last and most interesting of the lords was Reynard de Chatillon, known as 'The Elephant of Christ' (surely it should have been 'The Fox'?), who married the castle heiress Etienette de Milly, 'La Dame de Krac'. He was ruthless, cruel, brave and traitorous. He led his army to victory against Saladin (Salah al Din, who, incidentally, was a Kurd) at Montgisart in 1177, but lost the Battle of Hittin in 1187. As he had just raided a Muslim pilgrim caravan on its way to Mecca, breaking an agreement with Saladin, Saladin personally beheaded him with one swipe of his scimitar. In the period between, Saladin besieged the castle several times. During one siege, in 1183, a marriage took place between Reynard's stepson, Humphrey IV of Toron (aged seventeen) and Isabella (aged eleven), daughter of Queen Maria Comnena. The lady Etienette sent out some dishes from the bridal feast to Saladin. He, in turn, politely asked in which tower the nuptial couple were housed and gave orders that his siege weapons should avoid it: his nine huge mangonels bombarded the castle elsewhere until a Christian relief force arrived from Jerusalem. After the Battle of Hattin, Saladin's army besieged the castle again. It held out for eight months, under the command of Etienette, who must have been quite a girl. Saladin was so impressed with the bravery of the defenders that he released them. He gave the castle to his brother. By the time he died Saladin was able to leave his Ayyubid family a large empire stretching from Egypt to Asia Minor. Within sixty years it was lost – to slaves: the Mamelukes. These were Circassian slave soldiers founded by Saladin in the 1170s. They overthrew the Ayyubids in 1250 and became the Muslim rulers until conquered in 1517 by the Ottoman Turks under Selim I. After that the history of Kerak is tangled with the arguing and intriguing of the increasingly degenerate Ottoman factions. However, both the Saracen Ayyubids and Turkish-Egyptian Ottomans renovated and refined the castle, many repairs having to be undertaken after 1293 when a bad earthquake felled three towers and cracked much walling.

As I drive over undulating farmland the castle rears up on its rock bastion. Its walls are built of huge blocks of beigy-grey limestone. My guide book is out of date (*Guide to Jordan*, published in 1954, by The Franciscan Printing Press) and its illustration of Kerak shows a ragged sprawl of ruin on the top of cliffs, crumbling revetments and a small huddle of houses below it – not unlike pictures of the great monastery of Lhasa in Tibet. But now it has lost its desolation: there are many more houses; a macadamised road zigzags from below the castle to disappear into the town beside it; fallen blocks of stone have been replaced; the steep revetments have been so well restored that they are not unlike the retaining banks of a huge dam.

In Crusader times the only entrances were subterranean tunnels but I can enter through an Arab-built door at the far north end. The first impression inside is of an irregular jumble of walls and enclosures at different levels, here and there is the dark opening of a tunnel or gallery. Heaps of rubble have spilt from broken walls. There are well-like holes to rooms and tunnels below. The Norman arch is dominant in doorways or as vaulting. There are many arrow-slit windows. The ground underfoot is of loose gravel. Some wild rocket is flowering upon it – delicious and peppery, although a bit dusty and gritty on the teeth. There are many small irises about four inches high, none yet in flower; perhaps they are the black iris, which is the national flower of Jordan.

The plan in my guide book is simplistic: it shows that Kerak is trapezoid in shape, with the broader edge to the north, tapering to the south; it is surrounded by cliffs on three sides, with the dry moat on the north side. Only three places are itemised: a barracks in the north, a chapel in the centre, and the keep in the south. It says, but does not show, that the castle is built on seven separate levels; in addition the rock is pierced with tunnels and well sinks. So it is with a large amount of ignorance that I potter about: I look through the slit windows and speculate where the enemy would approach, and what I would do with my spear or arrows; I walk down a flight of steps into a long tunnel, four paces wide, which disappears into the darkness; stone cells are to either side, lit from above by small holes built into the ceilings, with mellow beige light, fading into gloom; I reach more rooms, some with flights of steps going further down into the dark; somewhere are dungeons. This place is a schoolboy's paradise. I have reached a sharp corner, it has become very gloomy. I need a torch. Two German girls in front have one. One of the girls is wearing a strong, musky scent. I follow them, partly through their torch, partly through their smell. They've speeded up, and are looking worriedly over their shoulders. I must stop or I'll give them the willies, sniffing after them like some weird lecher.

Out again, poking and prying: it is all very muddly and confusing. It would be nice to be with an expert who could say: 'This is where the catapults would be put . . . this round room was once the mosque . . . here is the site of a chapel . . . these carved panels and stone bench are the remains of an Arab bath . . . in that sunken area the Mameluke palace was sited.'

My guide book says that Reynard de Chatillon used to throw his prisoners over the battlements, having first protected their heads in wooden boxes so that they would survive to feel every bone break as they bounded down the revetments. There is a worried American woman nearby, hanging on to the stonework and peering over the edge: 'Oh my, think of being tossed over here.'

I was actually thinking of tossing other people over, perhaps the world is divided into the tossers or the tossees.

A hoopoe flies below me; above, swooping and wheeling and squeaking, are swifts.

I have now reached the block of walling standing at the far south end: the remains of the keep. It is a splayed-out U, with seven slit windows set in Gothic-arched recesses. The scenery all around is of agricultural land merging into wadi-with-mountains; it is misty, with flying sand far away, but I can just discern a blue stain smeared on the valley floor: the Dead Sea.

I am now on one of the lower courtyards, with a long line of slit windows behind me; in front is the bare rock over which the castle sprawls, like an octopus enveloping a bit of reef. The rock looks almost edible, in neat bands of nougat and chocolate, about five inches thick: alternate layers of limestone and chert, the latter sometimes containing little cells of quartz crystals, or rings within rings – like chert's close relation, flint. I can find no fossils in either type of rock.

I drive away, due west, with the great castle looming above my back. As I progress down the road, which meanders in and around knolls and hillocks and dells, the powder-blue-green expanse of the Dead Sea grows larger as I round each corner. I reach the flat of the plain that was once part of the sea bed. Somewhere, under the waters beside me, lie the remains of Sodom and Gomorrah. All that is left as their memento is a little chapel somewhere up the hill to the east, marking the cave where Lot was made drunk and seduced by his daughters, who thought that they were the last people left in the world. There is no time to look for it.

Apart from bedouin settlements, there is not much habitation: their tents are long and low, some black, some beige, mostly a dark chocolate-brown; their shacks are made from corrugated iron and wooden panels off packing cases.

What I thought was foam and spray from the sea turns out to be the shoreline rocks covered with dried salt. People are bathing in the sea – all men, wearing long, baggy bathing shorts down to the knee. After they get out of the water white patches of salt appear on their bodies as they dry.

There are narrow, deep slits, some maybe a hundred feet deep, cut into the plateau by rills and streams.

By the time I get back to my hotel, I have driven 373 kilometres in all, and deserve the large dinner I am about to eat.

Mr Julius Dikkop

Cavendish Square
London

1948 ~ London. Mr Dikkop was the bane of my childhood. He was a South African, with huge muscles developed during his time as a gold miner. Many professionals like to disguise their offices: you may enter a lawyer's and from his walls will assume that he is a salesman in rare prints; an architect's meeting room may look more like a West End club, an estate agent's like a library. Not Mr Dikkop, you knew where you were immediately you entered his torture chamber. The most terrifying thing about the many terrifying things in this room were the contents of a glass-fronted cabinet: an array of gleaming instruments – nippers, grippers, pliers, awls, knives, picks and prongs – all artfully arranged to either side of a human skull. This grinned nastily back at one, its teeth encrusted with bits of metal: rivets, fillings, bridges, braces and whatnot.

Yet in spite of his muscles and his array of instruments it took him over ten minutes and the handles of two teaspoons to lever out my governess's false teeth. She hadn't taken them out for twenty-five years.

Mr Ernest Throstle
Director

Simplex Stationery Co. Ltd
Spondon
Derbyshire

1986 ~ Lima. My first job in civilian life was in the engineering department of a huge textile factory in Derbyshire, and for my first task I was given a tape-measure and told to measure the distance of all the company-owned railway lines within the factory complex. My supervisor told me I had three days. I did it in ten minutes. Having done a spell in the army when a terrific song-and-dance was made about a sacred cow called 'Initiative', I used my highly honed enterprise: instead of walking all over the factory with the measuring tape, I used a foot rule – on a blueprint of the factory layout. I still remember the answer: 9 miles, 450 yards. My supervisor, a foreman, was rather disapproving of this, suggesting that I had a 'flippant attitude'; what I remember most about him were his extraordinary eyes, yellow, like a cat's. Perhaps, on analysis, they were a very, very pale tawny, but they looked yellow to me. There were about a dozen similarly-eyed people among the 27,000 who worked in that mill. The only other time I have seen eyes like that was at an embassy reception in Peru. A visiting businessman from Britain was there, trying to sell schoolbooks and stationery. He had yellow eyes. 'Interesting,' I said, 'I've only seen eyes the colour of yours when I worked in Derbyshire.'

'I'm a Derbyshire man, born and bred,' he said.

> Jean-Pierre du Barbet
>
> 66, Avenue des Tessiers
> Biarritz

1960 ~ Biarritz. 'Every cloud has a silver lining.' My maternal grand-mother served a fifteen-year stretch in a Parisian prison and, although this rather distressed my mother, it was quite a relief for my father. By the time her sentence was completed Grandmère had taken a dislike to Paris and went to live in Biarritz. There she made many friends – particularly men (which partly had been the cause of her absence from the social scene). One of them was du Barbet, a retired brigadier. His father had been a general and when going to war was accompanied by his valet, groom, chef, mistress-maidservant and personal photographer. Du Barbet had volumes and volumes of the resulting photographs, but what were particularly interesting were the movies. We would sit in the old brigadier's little drawing-room, and the heavy velvet curtains would be drawn. He would play and replay the battles of long ago: the shadowy outlines of the ranks of dead men rose to their feet

[177]

and ran and stumbled and fell as ghosts doomed to die again and again; their bodies had long ago rotted but their agonies lived on, revived by a ray of light through a strip of quaking celluloid. And the brigadier and Grandmère would chainsmoke and wax nostalgic of the Glory that had been France.

1999 June ~ CUBA, Havana

What do you give to someone who has been without any luxury for thirty-three years? When I was a child, during the war, the things people talked longingly about were stockings, chocolate, oranges and bananas, but my mother seemed to think that there were five other essentials: she kept an (illegal) hoard of sugar, tins of sardines, candles, matches and lavatory paper (Bronco) in the cellar. I cannot take too much for old Rose, or the customs officers will notice and nick; some luxuries in England are common in Cuba, tropical fruit and spices, for example. What I eventually choose are:

> three extra-large blocks of fruit-&-nut chocolate
> a jar of strawberry jam and a jar of blackberry jam
> a large chunk of cheddar cheese
> a box of three lily-of-the-valley scented soaps
> a pack of Swan Vesta matchboxes
> a pack of a dozen 'Biro' pens
> some copies of *The Spectator*, *The Week* and *Private Eye*.

The last choice may seem to be a bit odd, but a magazine full of criticism of governmental and other authority could be a delight and an amazement for someone who has seen no criticism of authority for three decades.

Rose says she is an historical relic: 'I am BC – Before Castro.' She looks to be in her mid-seventies: rather governessy; spectacles, crisp linen suit; grey hair cut neatly shortish and waved, well-kept teeth and fingernails; still handsome, may once have been very pretty; hobbles a bit, as she recently cricked her back lugging pails of water from the downstairs tap to her flat on the third floor. 'Everything breaks down in Havana, the electricity several times a day, now it is the plumbing, for the last week my apartment block has been without water except for that tap.' Her family had been lawyers and judges and she applied to read law in the university after 'BC' so that she could earn some money. But it was decreed that her 'type' must not go to university and so she has made her living by teaching Spanish to members of the diplomatic corps and visiting businessmen, and English to some of her country-men. Her English is good but her accent is an exaggeratedly articulated mouthing, as if she were adjusting her teeth with each word: 'Your English language is easy to teach, except for your dreadful spelling. We pronounce every letter in each word, which is why we sound so precise when we speak your language. If any Englishman wants a hearty laugh he asks us to say "Worcestershire sauce" or "Bournemouth".'

When Castro and gang overwhelmed the island most of Rose's friends and relations, the upper classes of Cuba, upped and fled like a tidal wave to the mainland of the USA. Rose herself stayed behind to nurse her dying mother, who took so long to die that Rose was left stranded, an isolated bit of jetsam on an unfriendly beach.

'It must be rather nasty for the likes of you?'

'It was not good to start with. They called my caste "worms", because like worms we were white, and crawled on our stomachs (to the Americans). My last extravagance was to have a brooch made in the shape of a worm. I wore it always, until they began to admire me for it. It is not too bad now, people are quite kind to this old woman, but they are all lower class and have no manners: they stand aside to let me pass with my full bucket, but they do not think of carrying it for me.'

Rose is acting as my guide today. Don, from the embassy, is kindly taking the day off to drive us about in his car.

Rose snuggles down in her seat: 'This is exciting, I have not been in a car for a long time. Of course in the old days I had my parents' chauffeur. How he would grumble after dances, when I would make him stop so that I could chase fireflies! I had my own car later, but had to sell it as I had no dollars or "chits" to pay for fuel. It was a beautiful Buick.'

'You must have got a good price for it?'

'No. You cannot sell to people. Anything you sell, be it a car or your dead mother's clothes, has to be to a government agency; this fixes the price.'

Don drives us down the Malecón, the seaside road lined with arcaded houses. I have not been to Havana for over two years. There is a noticeable change in its appearance and demeanour. It is like a woman beginning to put on make-up and a pretty dress after a long spell in prison. Everywhere scaffolding encages buildings: plasterers reface walls and mould ornamentations; joiners are replacing doors; masons work on flagging and carvings; painters paint; glaziers glaze; tilers tile. After the dramatic withdrawal of Russian sponsorship and subsidised importing, eighty per cent of Cuba's foreign trade vanished. There was terrific poverty and discontent; the country almost ground to a halt. So then, with great reluctance, Castro had to 'make a pact with the devil': to admit that the capitalist world would have to help, by spending money as tourists. He applied for international aid – and received it: Unesco declared Old Havana a designated area, and thus it gets money for repairs and maintenance; the Spanish government has given several millions for the Malecón to be renovated, 'much of our taxes are being spent repairing things denigrated for years as "evidence of the extravagances of the old bad days".'

The motto of the Cemeterio de Colón democratically says: 'Pale Death enters both Hovels and Palaces', but most of the incumbents seem to have been culled from the palaces. Rose proudly says that this cemetery is one of the three great ones in the world, the other two being in Paris and Geneva. To me it is not as impressive as the Cemetery of Recoleta in Buenos Aires, which is an even greater municipality of tombs-cum-chapels: but it has the same nasty, musty smell, and the same sad ambulators, looking forlorn and at a loss as they wander under the trees and along the grave-lined paths.

We start at the tomb of Rose's family. It resembles a large marble bed. 'I should be buried here, but I am beginning to dislike it. I am 'patrimonio' to several other tombs, a sort of guardian for families who were friends and who are in exile: on Mother's Day I have to put flowers on so many graves I need a wheelbarrow to carry them. I may have myself cut into pieces so that I can be buried in all the graves of which I have propriety.'

We walk past Gothic chapels, a Nazi pillbox in black marble, Doric mausoleums, Baroque sepulchres, a huge chunk of granite with Art Nouveau doors of bronze angels and flowers. Some tombs are like rooms full of filing cabinets; others are set about with angels and saints. Rose seems to have known every inhabitant: 'Her husband was my father's best friend . . . This was a great crook, not exactly a thief as he stole only from the government . . . Here's another great crook, but what style he had! What panache! . . . I knew this family so well and now none are left in Cuba . . . This next family traced themselves back to the aristocracy of Catalonia, now all that remains is this old woman, me, their family by proxy . . . A little sinister, these two, they both smiled a lot, but I never saw either of them laugh . . . Mafia, these ones, they should not be buried here, they should have gone back to their place of origin . . . A parvenu, this man, he was a *nouveau riche* yet he put lions at his entrance gates, a privilege reserved for only the best families. So the good families in his road removed their lions, as a gesture. It seemed all so important then, in the days BC.'

One grave is especially busy: heaped with wreaths, surrounded by young couples. 'The woman in there died during childbirth, she was buried with her baby at her feet; when the grave was opened both bodies were perfectly preserved and she was holding her baby in her arms. She is known as the Miracle Lady and many barren people leave flowers and ask for a baby.'

'So there are still remnants of religion?'

'Castro has never managed to get rid of it completely. A man in our block is a builder. He had a wooden roof strut, cross-shaped, too big to go into the truck, so he walked up the street with it on his shoulder. When he looked back he saw he was being followed by a large and devout procession.

'Similarly, Castro has not managed to destroy all affection for the United States. Although the US is the scapegoat and all our troubles are blamed on the blockade, the American people are well liked, many come here via Mexico and get a good reception. A boy in our street is named Oooess-navee (US Navy), but his sisters are Marlin (Marx-Lenin) and Chélee (Ché-Lives).'

Don drives us on, to a house once lived in by family friends of Rose's family: the Counts of Revilla de Camargo. It is now a Museum of Decorative [confiscated] Arts.

'I used to arrive here in a chauffeur-driven car,' she mourns, 'now I am not allowed in unless I am accompanied by foreign visitors.'

The garden is divided up into terraces and patios.

'Here I danced, among the statues, when I was a girl . . . Here the band used to play, by the fountain . . . I remember reproving my partner, a young Argentinian grandee, for throwing his cigar into this pool; there were fish in it then, and floating flowers . . . Here I gave a lily each to the three young men who were fighting to dance with me . . . it was fun in this house, long ago, when I was a girl, and people thought me beautiful . . .'

The interior is full of the type of furniture I dislike most: French Rococo. There are a lot of ormolu-encrusted, bulbous-bellied bits of furniture standing about on skinny little legs, and podgy cherubs and tapestries of bogus medieval hunting scenes, but there is an 'English Room' with some good Georgian and Regency furniture, and some excellent porcelain and silver.

There is a fountain in a niche in the dining-room.

'When we dined here, the fountain would play to cool the room and by its noise, to stimulate the conversation,' Rose says. 'Not that I needed any prompting, my mother said I never stopped talking and should remember that to flatter a man, a girl must listen – however stupid and boring he may be. But flattering men was never my priority – though *being* flattered perhaps was.'

The furnishing reminds me of my family's time in Eltham Palace. For the past five years English Heritage have been asking Dr Shirley Rodden, the archivist of Courtaulds Ltd, and me, and other members of my family about the furniture, fittings and equipment which Stephen and Ginie (Courtauld) had installed when they took over the place in the 1930s. This week it is being opened to the public and I have the catalogue-cum-guide. The opulent ostentation is astonishing. Cousin Ginie's bathroom, for example, is designed by Malacride. 'It has a vaulted ceiling and walls lined with onyx and embellished with black slate disks on to which were set glass spheres. The bath has gold-plated taps and a lion's-mask spout. It sits within a gold mosaic niche containing a statue of Psyche.' Some people have said 'how vulgar', but Stephen and Ginie couldn't care less. They had the attitude of Osbert Lancaster's Maudie Littlehampden who said, as she ate peas off her knife: 'As far as I'm concerned, if it's me, it's U.' The important thing which Stephen and Ginie did was to commission and encourage the very best of modern artists and craftsmen. In comparison, this Cuban house has many of the best names of the antique and collectors' world – Aubusson, Boudin, Chippendale and Sheraton, Sèvres, Meissen and Wedgwood, de Lamerie, Lalique – but nothing at all Cuban, except for the doors, of the local mahogany, beautifully carved, demonstrating what skills and materials were available should they have been used. What a waste of money and talent!

I comment on this to Rose. She replies: 'The trouble was that most of the Spanish could not face the truth that they were mere colonials – rustics, and they tried to make themselves courtiers and grandees of a Little Spain out here in the tropics.'

On to Fifth Avenue, lined with expensive houses and with a central strip of flowerbeds, topiary and flowering trees.

'This is Castro's show place, where all the foreigners are taken.'

It is certainly attractive. Well-tended gardens are set about the old-style villas, still spick and span, being the headquarters of international organisations or embassies. There are two noticeable exceptions. The first is a modernistic building, grim and gaunt, with a strangely humanoid tower: 'to keep watch over everyone – the Russian embassy. It is called "the robot". A Russian is called a "bollo" – which means "bowling ball" – after the shape of his head.'

The second exception is the ruin of a once-elegant villa. The garden is a mixture of unkempt trees which overshadow a scrubbery of bolted bushes, dead shrubs and tufts of grass and weeds. Much of the roof, gabled and turreted, has shed its cover of glazed green tiles so that rafters show like the ribs of a desiccated corpse. Windows stare blindly; doors gape; gutters have drooled down the walls which are blotched and cracked. Inside it is full of beautiful stuff: family pictures, carpets, furniture, all wood-wormed, mildewed, rotten. Among this sad decay live two old sisters, like Miss Havishams in a self-inflicted purdah motivated by nostalgia and resentment.

A side road is avenued with flambeau trees. They are all in flower and it seems as if we are looking down a tunnel of fire. In drab comparison, down another side street, there is a large queue by a shoe shop. 'Surely *all* those people don't want shoes?'

'You learn to buy whatever is available, you don't wait until you need it.'

We pass the elegant façade of a large building set back in well-tended grounds. 'That is a sports club. I used to belong to it, and used to come here often. It is where we danced on my fortieth birthday; that was in the old days, the days BC.' So, that means she is at least eighty-two.

'It is not for people like me now, it is for the Young Communists.'

'The night-clubs here are very good,' Don says.

'I wouldn't know. The night-clubs in Havana are all for foreigners. We Cubans are second-class citizens in our own country. I saw a television programme on 'Old' Havana some time ago, and I felt heartsick. I am not allowed there any more, unless I have a permit, it is only open to tourists and the new Cuban "aristocracy".

'In the days BC, for some of the peasants, particularly in the country-side, life was not good, very few schools or hospitals, and some of the rich people treated the peasants very badly: not just with indifference, but with cruelty. Also Havana became notorious as a centre of corruption and sin, ruled by the American Mafia. But life was good for people like me. But now there is a different aristocracy. There are three grades of the élite. Firstly there are Castro's men: the upholders of authority, the secret police and informers, the ordinary police (who are well paid as they are not popular), the Young Communists, the newspaper people and other spreaders of propaganda. Secondly the sportsmen and musicians who create international prestige. Lastly, the people with US dollars. These are the real "Haves"; everyone without dollars are the "Have-nots"; chambermaids are the Ladies and Baronesses, airline pilots are the Dukes and

Counts, everyone wants to work on international airlines or for the tourist business. The bare necessities are rationed – I am allowed four chickens a year – if the shop from which I must buy them ever has any. Only the dollar will buy anything else: the "Dollar-shops" for tourists and diplomats and officials will sell anything. Some officials get partly paid in chits which are "nominal dollars". But if you have a dollar the local CDR may find out and report you to HQ. Everyone tells on their neighbours.'

By CDR she was referring to the Comités de Defensa de la Revolución, official 'vigilant' groups serving as sneaks on their neighbours.

We are now in the state of Pinar del Río, driving down the six-lane 'autopista' which goes south-west down the tail of the crocodile-shaped island; the coasts are about twenty kilometres to either side of us. It is almost bare of vehicular traffic. There are people on horseback, and the local passenger carrier is rarely the car, but a light conveyance of a two- or three-seater bench on a light, tubular frame, similar to that of a racing trotter; there are traps and tumbrels pulled by mules and donkeys. Under every bridge, in the shade, hitch-hikers hopefully wait. Sometimes we pass open-backed lorries, packed with people and bicycles. We pass an improvised bus made from an old railway carriage which has been bolted on to the back of a truck; another railway carriage is alongside a cottage and is serving as a greenhouse.

The sugar plantations do not seem as well-weeded or fertilised as the ones I have seen in other parts of the Caribbean: the plants are thin and pale; in the scraggy remains of what seems to be an abandoned plantation, cattle and horses graze. Oxen are ploughing in some fields.

Candelaria, Las Peraszas Terrazas, La Moka. 'Where are we now, Rose?' Don asks.

'I have no idea.'

'But you are meant to be our guide!'

'I know. But everything has changed. I've never been on this road. No matter, if we are completely lost I will ask the way.'

We pass the ruined entrance of a once-rich estate.

'I know those gates,' Rose says, 'this place once had an English

name, but it had to be changed. At the end of BC no English words
were allowed, even words like "telephone" or "baseball". That rule is
usually ignored, but many such rules have been made, like the one
which commands that no man may have a beard like Fidel's.'

She nibbled at a bit of chocolate, then continued: 'A great evil of
power is the over-use of it for unimportant things; the impulse which
makes almost all rulers want to make rules: the tyranny of the Petty
Minded. And Castro is no exception. Yet he is clever. But he never
accepts advice, far less criticism, anyone who dares to criticise – even
friends – is never accepted again. And he is subtle at winning over
people, he has investigators who study all the people he is to meet, and
they tell Castro about these visitors' interests and problems and
opinions, so he wins arguments as he has the statements prepared,
and he knows what charms people. He has great charisma: when he
talks, and he talks often and lengthily, people listen and say: "That is
true, it is all the Americans' fault with their embargoes, and life is
better than when we were ruled by crooks paid by the Americans, and
there was no education and health care and this and that." Then Castro
stops talking and the people go home and reality returns, and they see
how much better the rest of the world is in comparison to us poor
Cubans.'

We are on the foothills of a mountain range, the Serria del Rosias.
The signs of agriculture dwindle and then vanish; the land around us
is covered with a dense growth of glossy-leaved vegetation and
palms.

We turn off the main road and go up the drive of an old coffee
plantation, once owned by family friends of Rose's family. As we
approach, the narrow lane becomes hemmed in by avocado, guava,
paw-paw, mango, all fighting to live within the tangled chaos of what
was once an orchard and formal garden: the once-pampered domestic
plants now being overwhelmed by the hardier local growth.

A mazy group of walls and paths indicates that we have reached the
plantation buildings. The height above sea level here is 800 feet and we
can see both the Cuban shores – maybe thirty miles from side to side.
The view is over rolling valleys to the coastal plains. There is a lake far

off; everywhere are clumps or isolated stands of the royal palm – a shock of feathery leaves atop a thin, grey, smooth trunk, up to eighty feet tall. Vultures wheel above. One lands in a tree near us and instantly is transformed from a thing of beauty – two vast, flying, feathered fans – into a huddle of untidy plumage out of which peers a tiny, bald, wrinkled, bright pink head.

The site is dominated by a large bell, formerly used to send orders to the slaves. Many of the ruins are of roofless stone cells, windowless and small: the punishment prisons for slaves. Terraces lead uphill, to where the coffee was dried. Rose needs Don and me to help her up the flights of steps which lead from terrace to terrace: she seems pretty steady to me; I think she rather likes holding hands.

Don and I agree that an aroma, a trace of coffee, still percolates in the air.

'Nonsense,' says Rose, 'this place hasn't seen a coffee bean since 1895, when arsonists burnt it down, and it was decided not to rebuild as it could not compete against Brazilian coffee.'

We lunch in an official tourist restaurant further up in the mountains, overlooking a river, scratching at mosquitoes and eating the locally caught fish.

'What do you miss most, Rose, in this modern Cuba?'

'What do I miss most? My heart often aches for the old days; but perhaps much of my nostalgia is for my departed youth, and for the conversation and laughter of people compatible to me. Things have not really changed that much: once the rulers were powerful because they were selfish and corrupt, now they are selfish and corrupt because they are powerful.

'What I miss most is my family, and freedom of speech.'

GEORGE   COURTAULD

OHIO

Late eighteenth and early nineteenth century ~ America. The first member of my family to go to the Americas was Great-great-great-uncle Samuel, who 'having dissipated ye family fortunes in ye French metropolis' (according to a disapproving niece) became a 'West India Merchant', i.e. a slave trader. Instead of getting the just deserts of a man whose 'language is to me most shocking' (another disapproving niece), he married the rich daughter of the President of the Supreme Council of the Commonwealth of Pennsylvania and Captain General and Commander-in-Chief; as a result he died well respected, leaving behind the offspring whose descendants survive as my American cousins.

George, his brother and my direct ancestor, was a very different man. His personality was of utterly opposing extremes: he charmed everybody he met, yet many people, including his loving children, were exasperated by him; he had immense drive and initiative, yet he succeeded in almost nothing; he had great foresight, yet he was childishly naive; he had boundless optimism, usually about impractical and futile ventures, yet he despaired of his elder son, Samuel, ever being a success. (George died as a relatively poor man in America; Samuel died as the richest textile manufacturer in the world.) A strong radical, disapproving of the Monarchy, the Church of England and of other pillars of the Establishment, George welcomed – at first – the French Revolution. He had starry-eyed ideals about the newly formed United States of America; he went to America four times, a rare achievement for those days. His main intention there was to found a commune with every member owning part of the assets of the community: 'from each according to his abilities, to each according to his needs'. Nowadays these early American communes are known as 'Owenite Settlements', but it was possibly great-great-great-grandpapa who inspired Robert Owen into buying New Harmony in Indiana and thus starting up those famous – and generally unsuccessful – settlements. Certainly, George's communes never succeeded. The settlers, after seeing the boundless opportunities in 'the land of the free', would begin to chafe at the rules and restrictions of their regimented and spartan life and break away to start up on their own. Great-great-great-grandpapa would then return forlornly back to England and brood there until he got the entrepreneurial itch once more and would set sail to start upon yet another futile enterprise.

He enjoyed travelling, whatever the method. He was possibly the first person to have gone down the Mississippi from beginning to end; this he did in a small skiff. He travelled for six hundred miles in the newly founded state of Kentucky, looking for a good place to start up a commune: safe, fertile and without too many neighbouring Red Indians or Roman Catholics; finally his 'poor little mare dropped dead from beneath me'. Above all he liked going in ships.

Among the many surviving family letters of this period is one which he wrote to his son Samuel, urging him to come over to the exciting new country of America, and to bring his friends:

- June 30th 1818. At sea – Latitude 50°, W. Longitude from Greenwich about 13°. Sailed from Dublin May ye 11th.
- Near 70 persons on board, and *all* as well as on shore. We will say nothing of the *first* week.

To Mr. Samuel Courtauld,
Bocking, Essex.

My dear Sam . . .

QUARTERS
Should 8 to 10 persons travel, the whole Cabin of a considerable Merchant Ship would not be too large, even with a good 'State Room'. These are grand places, perhaps 6 feet by $4\frac{1}{2}$, and each contains 2 berths. It is not uncommon for the captain to have to relinquish the other State Room also, which is otherwise reserved for himself. In this case he has to sleep in another Hole – the Mate's State Room, which has no light but from under the door, and is at the foot of the Companion Stairs. He and his officers then must mess on the landing.

[189]

BEDDING

A good, small mattress and suitable pillow with 2 blankets, 2 pairs of sheets and pillow cases is the proper furniture for each berth. Each passenger should have a small trunk, a sufficient stock of linen and stockings etc. for 8 weeks. They should also have a cambric bag or two for soiled linen, etc. At the head of every berth there should be a shelf with a pewter basin, a small tin Japanned jug and a horn cup. The cabin should be provided with a lamp and stand (to warm gruel, etc.). A large tin kettle or cask to contain one day's water for the party should be hung in some convenient situation, with a tap in the ladies' room and another in the general room.

WATER AND LIQUOR

It is very important that they should receive an allowance of water daily rather than receive an offer to use it as they find needful. The latter method will almost assuredly prove unsatisfactory both to the captain and to the passengers, and would probably occasion a needless consumption of this precious article. Half a pint of water is sufficient, with good management of the towel, to wash face, head, hands and feet etc. of one person; yet we know how easily a gallon may be expended for these purposes, and unless an allowance be given, the Master of a Vessel will always grudge fresh water being us'd for any species of washings.

2 quarts is our present allowance daily . . . Our water is now very sour, so that tea and coffee are nauseous, but chocolate completely hides the imperfection.

No one should embark a family without satisfying himself of the quantity on board being ample for the number of the ship's company. I apprehend 80 gallons for each person is not too much, allowing for accidents, the bursting of casks, long passage, etc.

Small quantities of white wine, not sweet but sound; I think good home brewed would do as well, also of spirits; brandy or whisky does as well.

[190]

Bottled porter is generally found to be the best drink at dinner for almost everyone after the first usual sickness may be over. Allowing one bottle to serve 2 persons one day, and allowing for 60 days and some breakage, 3 dozen for each person would be ample.

After more lists of food, spices, medicinals, drink, hardware and other equipment, the letter continues:

If the cabin table be well secured, and there be cleats on the floor to stop the hind feet of the chairs, the passengers will be sufficiently prepar'd for considerable tossing without much inconvenience from their furniture. A dozen common tablecloths may serve very decently for the passage by some soft rollers lash'd across the table to raise the leeward side of the dishes and plates.

By these precautions to render the family in a great measure independent of the caprice and ill humour of often a low bred Tyrant who is necessarily invested with absolute power, a summer voyage is more likely to be tolerably comfortable and even pleasant. Yet whilst the passengers should guard against all unpleasant interference of their Despot Chief, they must be aware that it will still be wise, whatever his character, to conciliate by polite attention. A female servant not likely to be long indisposed by sea sickness should certainly form one of the party, and express stipulation should be made with the captain for the full use of the cabin boy at immediate command, without any intervention from the captain, as well as occasional assistance from the cook; but they would do well to depend chiefly on themselves for cooking.

Wood and coals to be provided by especial agreement, with use of the caboose [galley].

I have no room for any other subject, so with all good wishes and affectionate love to all,

Yours,

G.C.

[191]

N.B. After the first week scarcely anyone was ill in the roughest weather (stiff breezes with a lumping swell) so that really sea sickness is not so alarming. In balancing the pros and cons of a remove, sea sickness should be considered but as dust in the scale.

Samuel was not cajoled. Though born an American, in the city of Albany, in the state of New York, once he had sailed from the barely chartered shores of the New World he never returned. In spite of his success – or perhaps because of it – Samuel riled his normally loving and tolerant father. Their characters were very different. George was a jovial, scatter-brained extrovert, Samuel a shrewd, shy introvert. In a letter to his eldest son George says:

> endeavour to throw off a certain stiffness and distance of manner, which is apt to chill first impressions of benign affections . . . In addition to [your] bolt upright figure . . . you usually add an unnatural kind of broad grin, which seems to arise from a forced attempt to look pleased. This grin disfigures an intelligent and manly face, the natural expression of which is that of serious thoughtfulness.

George also had trouble with a stubborn wife. He had met Ruth (née Minton) while she was in America with her brother. She was Irish, very pretty with long black hair and a cream complexion, and had been brought up in comfort on her father's estate near Kanturk. They married in 1789, 'in a house on the Mohawk River'. They left America soon after their marriage. George returned alone, and lured her back to him only once.

When reading his letters to her, I began to realise that, perhaps, he did not really want her to rejoin him. Is the following letter subtle, or guileless? It was written to Ruth during his last visit to America and purports to persuade her to return to him and their two younger sons, George [II] and John.

8th March, 1821.

> Englishtown,
> Near Athens, Ohio.

I am in a small room built of logs, plastered inside and out with sand; it has a ledged door, through the cracks of which – from its shrinking – a mouse, unless very young, could not pass; the floor being also made of green boards is now so open that my doubled fist can easily pass between them; but this imperfection is of *small* importance, as having well filled-in the walls of the house, no cold air rises from below, nor do we experience much inconvenience from knives and brushes, etc., falling through, for as these boards are not nailed, we have only to lift one of them and pick up what had fallen; sometimes it is not done immediately, so that after several little privations the boards are moved and we recover many lost friends all in a moment.

Our ceiling, or more properly our upper floor, is doubly boarded, which though it does not keep out the wind, prevents the wheat falling through from the loft. Our fireplace is of stone: that is, it is a case of wood lined with stone – 4 feet high – the upper portion of poles, the interstices filled in with sand: our hearth very rough stone, but we have the luxury of cast-iron andirons to prevent the wood rolling on to the floor: our loft might indeed have been honoured with the name of 'chamber', though certainly not all suited to shelter any animals superior to mice or birds; to this place we have a ladder, made by George and myself.

The furniture of our cabin, and its inside decorations, besides the aforesaid ladder, consist of two windows, shelves and open closets (some made of rough boards), some of our boxes set up on end or raised on their side, our baggage, trunks and boxes, placed round the room. Two tea chests full of books support your large flat trunk which serves as a kind of high table, and besides this we have a kind of drop table with a drawer – made of poplar – on which I am now writing with sufficient convenience (except when now and then one of the legs slips between the boards and throws off paper, pens, etc.). In one corner of our room we have our flour barrel, in another the bran, in a third a bar of salt; the fourth is occupied by our bedding. We have not yet the luxury of a bedstead; the bed George and myself sleep on is of straw. John sleeps between us and the fire on a buffalo skin – which is about as soft as our straw bed – and which serves also as his bolster; ours is formed by a roll of carpeting under the head of the bed. We have made ourselves very comfortable at nights through this severe winter by a kind of moveable screen and side curtains formed of sheets and blankets – and good fires.

The walls of our room are ornamented with steel-yards, scales, mops, broad-sword, fire arms, saws, axes, mattocks, candles and candle moulds, and jugs, bowls, and the whisky bottle – the latter very sparingly used, I assure you, by ourselves, but I believe to be one of the good things given us moderately to enjoy.

We have not yet been able to procure a chair, and therefore have contented ourselves with two 3-legged stools. John had one with 4 legs which is now broken; but we find plenty of seats, and when we have visitors we borrow one of the two long forms which are part of the furniture of our common room. I first called this my 'private room', but having experienced that all callers found free admission into it, I called it our 'store room'; but as the word store here means shop – and as all shops are public rooms – it produced an increase in visitors until we found I had nothing to sell, except a crate of earthenware . . .

Great-great-great-grandmamma stayed in England with sensible son Sammy.

1999 July ~ OMAN

I was 'retired' as a Queen's Messenger fourteen months ago. And here I still am, on the routine journey to Muscat and Oman. My Omani Arab friend is away on holiday so I have rented a car. The driver-cum-guide is a bag of bones with a sad moustache; he has affected a studious mien with gold-rimmed spectacles and a dun-coloured cardigan of the baggy shapelessness favoured by prep-school masters in days of yore. He says his name is Edmundo De Souza. 'Portuguese?' I ask. A melancholy smile flitters under the moustache: 'Indeed, my family were once thus, when the Portuguese were masters of the eastern seas under Vasco da Gama and Affonso d'Albuquerque. My ancestors settled in Goa, which is the State of my origination.'

In 1498 Vasco da Gama rounded the Cape of Good Hope and as a result the Portuguese dominated this part of the world, the Persian Gulf and the Indian Ocean, from 1507, when they captured Muscat, to 1650, when they were expelled. Many of the fortifications in Oman are either of Portuguese origin or influence. I have all day spare and plan to visit a couple, the best in the mountains to the south-west of Muscat, where I am based.

Edmundo is driving us along the main road between Muscat and Sohar, along the coastal plain called the 'Batinah': 170 miles long by about eight wide, but with a narrower strip actually under cultivation. 'Observe,' Edmundo says, 'oil money is being spent lavishly on beautification': alongside the road gardeners water and weed and tend mile after mile of topiary trimmed from bougainvillaea, and lawns, flowerbeds, urns and trees – mostly palms. Further inland I can see the more practical orchards and market gardens and even further into the boulder-strewn gravel of the Batinah grow the poor country cousins: spiny shrubs, flat-topped bushes, contorted trees, all dusty and dry and sparsely spaced out in the dry ground.

The houses are dazzlingly white, most are well designed; there are many mosques, with domes like Easter eggs and minarets like salt-shakers. We pass the complex of the university; Edmundo tells me that there are 3600 undergraduates, sixty-five per cent of them female: 'only fifteen years ago persons of the female gender were not permitted to have any formal education.'

After forty miles, at Barka, we turn left and head for the mountains. A sign indicates that our next destination, Nakhl, is twenty miles away. The heat is intense. The road shimmers in mirage and the few approaching vehicles appear as if hovering over the surface.

*   *   *

The castle-fort of Nakhl stands beside its village with an impressive backdrop of the Jebel Akhdar – the Green Mountain Range. Last time I was in Oman I knocked at the castle door of the Lord of the Green Mountains. He was out.

Nakhl's castle-fort was the centre of the Ya'ruba tribe, famed builders of fortifications. It looms a hundred feet above us: six towers, with higgledy-piggledy walls and ramps and battlements seemingly plonked on a cluster of colossal boulders. It is constructed from the usual limestone basis with wood reinforcements and fittings and plastered with a mud and cement mixture of a lovely warm pinky-beige. The ornate wooden entrance door reminds me of Zanzibar, perhaps not surprising as Zanzibar was once a possession of Oman. Edmundo and I enter and we meander about on the stone paving of the interior, up and down flights of steps, through narrow passages and alleyways, across yards, into towers and rooms. Everywhere we stand we are overlooked by a defence wall or a turret, whose gun-slits point not only out at any potential enemy, but also inwards, should the enemy manage to break in. I am reminded of the lessons of intercommunicating defence the Crusaders learnt from the Arabs, and which were passed on – and here they are, back again. Sometimes the mother rock bulges out from a wall or rears through the flagging, to show that the building has been fused into its surroundings.

The temperature is now almost 50° C: it is so hot that my sweat is stinging and blinding me, my pen won't write on my sodden paper, and I cannot feel any air entering my lungs, so it is like being stifled in hot cottonwool. Yet Edmundo persists in wearing his cardigan; I think it has some special significance for him, either ceremonial or of status, like a morning coat at a wedding or a rugger player's jockstrap.

'You're not sweating,' I point out admiringly.

'I am very proficient at retaining my bodily fluids,' he informs me.

It is a relief to go indoors, out of the glare: there is a date store-room, a kitchen and a pantry; there are soldiers' barrack rooms, bathrooms, majlis (council rooms) guest rooms and living-rooms. Of these, the boys' are stocked with armaments and books; the girls' are full of fluffy things – dolls and cushions and hangings of fabric and cushions and suchlike – as are the women's with the addition of chests and china.

Inside some of the rooms there is the oriental arch, the ogee, somewhat similar to the Venetian one, with an angle-bracket-shaped top. As we ascend the rooms become cooler, 'because of the passage of air through the fenestration,' Eduardo says. The 'summer sitting-room' is well fenestrated: ten windows, five per side. The floor is covered with matting on which are three good carpets; cushions in horrible yellow satin are propped against the walls, with guns and khanjars (Omani daggers) hanging from them; there are niches storing china and books. The coolest room, at the very top, is the wali's (local ruler's) private sitting-room. Near it is a well, very deep: it is bored right through the castle, through the rocks upon which it is built, and into the water table. Eduardo and I stand in the highest tower, next to a cannon marked 'GR 1803' (presumably George III), and look over the shimmering, shaking fronds of hundreds of palm trees; the Green Mountains rear up behind, children's voices rise up from the flat-topped houses.

We left Nakhl at noon, bound for Rustaq, thirty-five miles away. Before we set off we went to a little shop and bought something to drink.

'Beer, cider, wine, tea, coffee, milk, when you are really thirsty nothing can beat a drink of very cold water,' I said to Eduardo.

'Water – apart from life itself – our Merciful Father's greatest bequest, I imbibe nothing else,' he said primly.

We drove through a rubble-scattered plain which became a wide wadi bed, the trace of the dried-up river being evident in rounded boulders and banks of gravel; the mountains changed from greenish to a chocolate brown, then became stained with ginger, red, pink, ochre, yellow and back to blue-green again. When a couple of miles from Rustaq we passed a tower on a hillock, surrounded by an oasis.

'What's that?'

'I knoweth not, perchance it is a village-oasis called Kasfah.'

'We might have a look at it later, if we have the time.'

He made no reply, but his sad moustache seemed to sadden.

Rustaq was once the capital of Oman. Like Nakhl, it is backed by a magnificent mountain range, this time an extraordinary pack of vast limestone slabs up to ten thousand feet high and set aslant like a stack of colossal books, they demonstrate the immense geological movements which caused the sea floor to rear up into the sky. The castle is called Qala'at Al Kesra and is the oldest in Oman, being originally built by the Persians in AD 600 – although it has been tittivated during the ensuing time so that now much of the building is of the early eighteenth century.

Edmundo drives us round the perimeter wall: 'It is ten metres high with over two thousand crenellations. Yet mere stone and mortar are not defence enough against the forces of the righteous. A virtuous mind and a noble purpose can overcome the most impregnable of defences.'

'Quite so.'

We enter and park in the shade of a clump of scraggy trees.

First, we inspect the water supply. The castle was built over a spring, the start of a 'falaj'. The falaj system was invented about 1000 BC. It is a method of transporting water through underground channels. The 'mother well' is dug into the water table, usually at a foothill of a mountain. Sinkholes are dug along the course to be taken, and then joined by underground tunnels; from the air, the sinkholes can look like a line of bomb craters. Whenever the tunnel surfaces it becomes channelled into a 'falat', and as it meanders through the open ground so an oasis grows around it, and a village is born, and usually a defending fort or watchtower. The flow of water is governed by strict regulations, sometimes its ration is allocated with the use of sundials. The water 'rights' are inherited like the 'gates' of sheep on a Yorkshire moor.

Just below the castle, water flows along a falat built from stone slabs. The water is of a beautiful translucent, blue-green-silver like willow leaves, though the colour is more likely to have leached from the green mountains whence it comes. It looks as cool and tempting as the moonbeams of Paradise, but when I put my hand in it, it feels as warm as blood. There are many little fish, drab-coloured but for tails with alternate bars of black and a vivid, electric blue. When they flutter their tails, this blue flashes and twinkles like tiny sparks from a striking flint.

As we enter the castle I look up and see muzzles of cannon poking out of the tower above me. 'There are four towers here – the Red Tower, Satan's Tower, Wind Tower and Al Hadieth,' Edmundo tells me.

'What does Al Hadieth mean?'

'That is not in my cognizance.'

'You speak very interesting English, Edmundo, where did you learn it?'

'Primarily, at St Xavier's. Now I make it a custom to peruse at least one page of the *Shorter Oxford Dictionary* before I lay me down to sleep.'

'St Xavier's?'

'A school run by monks, a – what is the male equivalent of a nunnery?'

'A monkery, perhaps?'

'Monkery! A word new to me! I shall add it to my repertoire.'

I feel a bit guilty.

Once again he and I potter and pry amid a maze of passages, tunnels, staircases and rooms. Here and there we come across channels of water from the falat: sometimes as a gleam in the gloom, sometimes as a reflection off an arched roof, sometimes as a faint movement far below. There are many musty, hot, unlit cells, often far down, with flights of steps descending to them. To my oft-repeated 'What's that?', 'Dungeon' is the invariable reply.

Two of the towers have cannon platforms. In one of these an upper floor is segmented into five cannon ports. The ceiling is beautiful, being held up by six arches. The cannon have neat piles of cannon balls beside them, not large, about the size of a grapefruit. Eduardo tries to pick one up. His skeletal fingers clamp upon it like the legs of a spider round a beetle. He heaves. It does not budge. He approaches it from another angle. It remains glued to the spot. He tries again. And again. And again. He demonstrates the same futile optimism as does my overweight pug when chasing swallows. He gives up. I look tactfully away.

Near the very top, from a paved roof-yard containing two tombs (of previous walis) and a well head, Eduardo and I look over the battlements at the oasis below, where about thirty thousand palms are growing. Eduardo says: 'Dates are Oman's biggest export, ten million palm trees produce 160,000 tons per year. The date, a nutritious fruit, comes in many varieties and is the staple diet of much of Arabia. Of greater significance, perhaps, is the use of its leaves in making crosses on Palm Sunday.'

We return to the unknown fort in the 'village-oasis which may be called Kasfah'. Eduardo and I reckon it is too big to be a watchtower, so it is probably a military fort (more businesslike and less of a residence than a castle-fort), built here partly to guard the water and the road, and partly to send advance warning of strangers to the main castle two miles away.

It is built on a knoll. The basic material is mud brick, reinforced by stone and wood. Around the base of the knoll there is a muddle of walls and cells. The dominant element atop the knoll is a large drum tower. It is in decay, like a huge chocolate cake melting in the sun.

We walk towards it through the village of shoddily built cement houses; as we near the fort, they become replaced by mud-built houses, mostly deserted. We enter the warren of alleyways and very narrow passages between cells and pits and walls which were once small inhabitations. Amid the ruins there is a surprising number of ornate wooden portals and doors: in England, by now, such things would have been ripped out, dewormed, polished and set up in the front windows of antique shops. The other artefacts are plastic, a littering of bags and water-bottles. There is a persistent smell of ordure. Having clambered and climbed, we have reached the steep and gritty banks below the drum tower and it is time to scramble and slither. Eduardo gives up: 'I am not attired in raiment suitable for such promenade,' but I make it up to the main doorway of the tower. It is half blocked by mud, which has flowed in globs like a flood of lava. Looking over it into the tower I see a chaos of fallen rafters and mud and stone. The whole place is subsiding back into the hill from which it was built. I lean against a wall and it rocks. It is dangerous here: something might fall on me, or I may disappear into some cellar or well. Time to go.

Eduardo drives us through the oasis, following the course of a large falat, in the dappled shade of palm trees where grow citrus trees – probably the famous Omani lime – mangoes, bananas and vegetables. We find ourselves back at Rustaq. Eduardo drives on, towards the coast.

The castle fort of Hazm is a few miles further on. It is severe, its rectangular outline dominated by a flag.

I tell Eduardo to carry on. It is now late afternoon and like Dominie's 'wat fatigue' in Thailand, I am getting 'fort fatigue'.

'Very fine and impressive, all these places,' I say to Eduardo, 'but I suppose in a few years' time they will only be useful as sites for tourists, and false myths and exaggeration will be woven into their histories.' I quote Neal Ascherson: 'Nostalgia makes bad history.'

'Maybe,' replies Eduardo, 'but perchance it may add some gold leaf to the cast iron of Truth.'

DASHO PASANG WANGI

(*Dzongdag Tongsa*)

1985 ~ Bhutan. The district of Tongsa is in central Bhutan. It is rarely visited by outsiders and the roads are rough. Much of the way is through rhododendron forest, at this time of year the shrubs are flowering: sometimes the globes of blossom are as big as pumpkins. To get to Tongsa our expedition had a long drive: ten hours, but that included many stops to look at plants and birds. We passed through a village called Nob-Ding: a good name.

One of the places we stopped at was stunningly beautiful even by the standards of Bhutan. The area was dominated by a *chorten*, which means stupa, or shrine. The *chorten* was like a tiered wedding cake in whitewashed stone. Large pairs of eyes were painted near the top, at each point of the compass. Flowering shrubs grew around it with such perfection of shape and excellence of spacing and grouping that one would have thought a hundred gardeners, not just God, had been involved in their planting and upkeep. A clear river ran alongside, redstarts and wagtails flew over its pure waters, scarlet rhododendrons and pearly willows leaned over them.

I paddled over to a shrubby island to examine some clusters of bright red tubular flowers growing in a bush: they were woodfordia.

Having arrived at our encampment overlooking the Tongsa Dzong (a *dzong* is a fortified monastery) in the afternoon I laid out my kit in my tent and then sallied out alone. I found a woody ravine a couple of miles away. There were many superb flowers within it, some I could identify from the book I brought with me, but I had to take samples from a few for the others to identify on my return. Because the climb out of the ravine onto the track involved the use of hands as well as feet I stuck the plants round the band of my trilby, much to the surprise of a wood-gatherer whom I met by the torrent. I had the greater surprise, however: although laden with a huge bundle of faggots on his back, he shinned up surfaces in front of me using just his bare toes for purchase, while I needed all the studs in my boots, plus all ten fingernails and, if it had been possible, my front teeth.

Two of my specimens stumped everyone for some time: they were both climbers, and both had a slight resemblance to some of the lesser-flowered clematis. The flowers were small, drooping, rather waxy bells, greenish on one plant and purplish on the other; both smelled strongly and pleasantly. We finally identified them as two species of holboellia. The most interesting plant was called an agapetes. I first saw it as a row of sealing-wax-red drops hanging from the underneath of a branch. On climbing the tree, I discovered that the inch-long flowers were aligned along the stem of a creeper. It is 'epiphytic', which means it grows on other plants but is not their parasite.

In the evening we were invited to the house of Dasho Pasang Wangi, Dzongdag Tongsa. Translated, this is Sir P. Wangi, Chief Commissioner, Tongsa District. He is perhaps a bit shorter than the average Bhutanese, but otherwise typical: Mongoloid, with slanting eyes, glossy black hair and a broad smiling face. Because of their clothes the Bhutanese appear, at first sight, to be akin to the Scots. The chief garb of the men is a belted gown which ends, kilt-like, just above the knees; below that they have long woollen stockings and sensible leather shoes. The gown is often patterned in tartan-like squares and checks; over this, some men throw a long plaid. The Dzongdag's gown has long white sleeves, to show that he is an important official. The women have a longer gown, reaching to the ground. It also is often in tartan patterns.

The interior of his house is in the same taste as the exterior: a pleasant muddle of carved and painted walls and woodwork; of dragons and curly haired, pop-eyed beasts, little religious statues and many small ornate tables and comfortable chairs and sofas. His pleasant and friendly womenfolk were in the room with us, so were a general and his wife. We ate crunchy handfuls of some sort of toasted grains, rice perhaps, and drank yak tea.

Next morning we accepted the Dzongdag's invitation to visit him at work: at eight o'clock, after breakfast. We went into the *dzong* where he has his office. He has a huge desk, brightly and gaudily painted with animals and curlicues. He sat behind it and we photographed him. While posing, he put on a stern and important expression. He showed us the wall charts which indicated costs and timings of the local construction jobs planned for the next few years: most of them were for roads and bridges; some were for hospitals and schools. One diagram showed the chain of command from the king right down to their equivalent of parish councils: the church committee was as important as the most senior civilian committee.

> *HIS HOLINESS the*
> *INCARNATION*
> *LLAMA of THYANGBOCHE*
> *NAWANG TENSING SANGPO*

1985 ~ Nepal. There are twelve of us trekkers, led by Nicholas Guppy. Our train of seven Sherpas has a *sirdar* (leader) called Pasang Temba. He is smallish and burly, with huge calf muscles on his rather bowed legs. He smiles broadly, with crinkly eyes, large teeth and shiny bunched cheeks. The other Sherpas range from the cheerfully youthful to the mournfully aged. The oldest is Ishi; he has two thumbs on one hand

and a wizened, sad face exactly like a chimpanzee which has lost its nuts. We have also ten dzooms to carry our baggage. Dzooms are crosses between yaks and domesticated cattle. They have good horns, are as hairy as highland cattle, and are either black or piebald; the males are 'mules', the cows fertile. They take the heavy loads, such as our tents; the Sherpas carry the lighter equipment.

The monastery of Thyangboche sprawls over a flattish, broad col about 12,500 feet above sea level, with a good view of Everest. The final phase of our walk up to the monastery was quite strenuous: for a couple of hours our climb was so steep that even the dzooms felt tired; I felt very guilty during my rests when they tottered past, their poor black tongues hanging out as they panted and drooled. During one of my pauses Lavinia, one of our party, came up on her pony, dismounted, and we discussed some of the fauna around us. Huge horseflies settled on her animal and I began to swat them. The Sherpas started tittering, shocked and embarrassed, I suddenly remembered that they are Buddhists and it is against their religion to kill anything. Sheepishly, but speedily, I desisted.

A ceremony was taking place when we arrived here about midday. The born-again Llama and his brother monks were on a high ridge above the monastery. They were beating drums, tinkling cymbals, chanting prayers and swilling tea from large thermos flasks. I was the last to leave and as I rose to go three monks, who had dug a deep hole in which to put the foot of a large flag-staff, asked me to help them raise the pole. With many a grunt we hauled it upright. I regretted that there was no-one there to photograph the picturesque scene. When I left to the goodbye waves of the monks, the prayer flags were fluttering high in the air, streaming out prayers like the pollen in a hay field.

We met the Llama of Thyangboche in his reception room, rather spartan with bare walls of pine planking and a few bookshelves. He was small, with a little round head covered with short grey fuzz, like a gooseberry. We had to bow to him with our hands clasped in greeting and then present him with white scarves, into the folds of which we had tactfully secreted some bank notes. He assumed a wary half-smile which Lavinia and Nicholas said gave him an appearance of great holiness and benevolence; I thought it made him look shifty and ill at ease. We sat on benches around the room and looked at each other in silence for some time. Nicholas then gave a formal oration to the Llama on the great honour we had in meeting him, how much we admired his country, his religion, his friendly kindness, his monastery, the holy simplicity of his bare pinewood panelling and the celestial awesomeness of his hill-top rite.

There was another longish silence.

Eventually the Llama said something to Pasang who turned to Nicholas and said: 'His Holiness says that his walls are unpainted as he has just had this room rebuilt.'

There was another pause. We then asked a few more questions, which he answered curtly. Pasang translated the curtness into lengthy and flowery passages. Most of our questions were pretty boring: had he been to Bhutan (which we had just visited)? where had he been born (the latest time)? did the monks do any farming? how old was he? – 463 and six reincarnations – but things became more interesting when he started talking politics. We had asked him what he thought about the Chinese in Tibet. He replied that many Buddhists and Tibetans wanted to return to Tibet, as the Chinese were saying that they were welcome and that they now regretted the destruction and looting of the monasteries. However, most people were frightened to go, as it was not possible to trust a communist. A nine-year-old monklet then handed round some coffee (surprisingly good) and biscuits (stale), the Llama asked for books on education and solemnly gave us each a long white scarf made from a loose-woven cotton, he said that it was a 'good-luck' scarf for travellers. Nicholas lectured him about controlled forestry, and we quit.

On our return here, to the camp far below the monastery, we heard a great hubbub and yells of laughter and excitement: Lavinia's mare had come into season and was being chased up and down the camp site and valley by a randy stallion.

Dinner was at 6.30, consisting of soup, tinned stew, cauliflower, vegetable noodles and tinned fruit salad, all washed down with tea – the best tea in the world: nutty, salted, with yellow globules of yak fat floating in it. As happens every evening, as we ate round the table in the main tent, we debated on three subjects: flora, fauna, and the workings of our insides.

Now I have snuggled into my sleeping bag. Sheet lightning is flickering amidst the mists and cloud-covered mountains, but there is no thunder. The battery of my torch is going flat. Someone is already snoring gently in the tent nearby, but the gin-rummy players are still laughing and arguing in the main tent. The dogs are beginning to bark. Now rain has started to patter on to the outside of my tent. This is bliss: I don't know why.

That long white scarf which the Llama gave me was tied to the bag I use on my travels. It has protected me for fourteen years, for three and a half million miles: in the terror-wracked streets of Monrovia, Luanda and Beirut; amongst the dolour and despair of Calcutta, Lima and Lagos; alone in the dead cities of Petra, Teotihuacan, Polonnaruwa and Fatehpur Sikri; amid angry, anti-British mobs in Santiago and Jamaica; facing bloody stupid border guards and customs officers everywhere; 36,000 miles of train journeys from Peking to Ulaan Baatar and back and, in aeroplanes, more dud take-offs and aborted landings than I care to remember.

Now my traveller's good-luck scarf is so worn and frayed that only about six inches are left. Time I gave it a rest.

But . . .